Clockwork Debt

Clockwork Debt

Trade and the External Debt of Developing Countries

Pierre Dhonte
Caisse Centrale de Coopération
Economique

LexingtonBooks
D.C. Heath and Company
Lexington, Massachusetts
Toronto

Library of Congress Cataloging in Publication Data

Dhonte, Pierre.
Clockwork debt, trade and the external debt of developing countries.

Bibliography: p. 117.
Includes index.
1. Underdeveloped areas—Debts, External. 2. Loans, Foreign, I. Title.
HG4517.D49 336.3'435'091724 79-1753
ISBN 0-669-02925-4

Published simultaneously in Canada.

Printed in the United States of America.

International Standard Book Number: 0-669-02925-4

Library of Congress Catalog Card Number: 79-1753

Contents

List of Figures

List of Tables

Introduction

Ten years ago the external debt of developing countries could be called the counterpart of "aid," a problem for borrowers and benevolent lenders. This is not the case anymore. Its accumulation has now grown into a commercial relationship in which industrial countries have as large a stake as borrowers: it has become central to world trade.

The primary indication of that sweeping change is the sixfold increase of the value of debt over the last ten years. The reality of the change runs much deeper, however: it lies in the rationale of that increase. The accumulation of debt in recent years was more than a response to the developmental needs of borrowers; it was a response—and an efficient one—to the disruption of established trade patterns following the oil crisis and the 1975 recession. As it saved developing countries a brutal curtailment of their imports, it also allowed industrial countries to offset a significant share of their oil deficit by a sizable trade surplus with developing regions. On that occasion, the accumulation of debt acquired a global significance and became essential to international adjustment.

It still is. The huge overhang of debts cannot simply be written off or paid back: it can only be rolled over, as new loans pile up to refinance the old ones. Should this fail, developing countries would have to curtail their imports, industrial countries would experience undesired deficits and restrictive policies could add up to a recession. The task, however, is not small: under the thrust of debt servicing, disbursements of new loans will soar from $40 billion in 1976 to $90 billion by 1980 and may well top $200 billion—annually—by 1985. The basic question, then, is not about the ability of developing countries to pay their debts: it is about their capacity to borrow.

A firm can borrow forever as long as its cash flow is growing in line. A country can do the same if its exports expand in proportion. The debt of developing countries will increase rapidly: will their exports follow? There lies the crux of the matter: the debt of developing countries cannot be managed unless their trade expands, and trade in turn cannot expand unless their debt is sustained. It is a clockwork; it can be geared for growth or recession.

After the oil shock, will there be a debt shock?

The Mechanics of Debt

An understanding of the dynamics of debt is required to avoid adverse developments. Debt has too often been argued about in allegoric fashion (the debt burden) or in idealistic terms (the pure "resource transfer"). All this ignores its very nature: it is indeed a way to channel resources to a borrower, but it is not an unspecific way. It has its own logic.

The logic of debt financing is to squeeze a net resource transfer out of large opposite gross flows. New loans must refinance the old ones before they cover the interest and add to the borrower's disposable resources. This requires a continual increase in disbursements and in debt outstanding; unless that increase proceeds at some minimum rate, not enough is left of new loans, after the old ones have been rolled over, to cover the interest payments, let alone to achieve a net transfer of resources.

On the other hand, the growth of debt and of disbursements cannot lastingly be out of proportion with that of the borrower's economy, and notably of its exports. Otherwise, confidence would be impaired, and the refinancing of outstanding debt would be jeopardized.

Basic to an understanding of debt is the fact that its growth rather than its level is the crucial issue. Unbalanced growth, not the level of debt per se, is the substance of excessive debt. The growth of debt can be neither so low nor so high as desired; unless the permissible ceiling exceeds the required minimum, the process becomes inconsistent and a crisis evolves.

The core of debt management is to run a course between these two pitfalls in a way that can be sustained indefinitely. This is more easily achieved when the terms are favorable, with long maturities and low interest rates; it is also easier to achieve when disbursements can increase strongly because of a powerful export performance. Together the terms of the loans and the borrower's export performance are essential to determine the capacity to borrow.

Commercial Lending versus Official Assistance

While the logic of debt has always been operative, the constraints which it imposes on debt management have increased in significance in recent years because of a profound change in the debt relationships. This change bears some analogy with the transition in industrial countries from the Marshall Plan to the Euromarkets. It has been made possible by the emergence, out of two decades of development, of a new class of developing countries: these are the middle-income developing countries, home of 900 million people, with an average per capita income of about $1,000 per year. These countries have achieved very high growth rates over the last fifteen years, much higher than those of industrial nations and very much larger than could be attained by the other low-income developing countries. In addition, they have developed a capacity to sustain high growth rates on their own resources with little or no foreign financial assistance, a result still out of the reach of the low-income countries, which are suffering from extreme handicaps. As a consequence, for all the uncertainty about the border cases, substantial differentiation prevails between these two groups, while the middle-income countries now have gained many of the features of developed regions.

This development is very significant because it has been matched with comparable changes in the structure of world trade. As recession was deepening in industrial regions, import demand by developing countries, sustained by heavy borrowing, exerted a stabilizing influence. While developing countries remain highly dependent on economic conditions in industrial countries, the reverse now also holds true possibly to a lesser, but significant and rising, extent.

The bearing of this new situation on international lending is that the borrowing activity of middle-income countries has become increasingly commercial in character. This is properly captured by the terminology of "commercial" and "aid-dependent" developing countries suggested by Beim.[1] Aid-dependent countries receive loans on concessional terms for assistance purposes; this was the backbone of international lending to the developing countries in the 1960s. Commercial financing is extended at market terms for commercial purposes; this has been the dynamic sector of lending activity over the last ten years.

It is easily seen how the development of commercial lending imposes more exacting limits on the accumulation of debt. Market terms are less favorable than those of official lending, which complicates debt management, while private creditors have less capacity than official agencies to cope with liquidity problems, so that a continuingly smooth rollover is all the more essential.

The Policy Options

The inflation of the 1970s has done much to erode the real weight of external debts, which is not currently much larger than it was at the turn of the decade. The momentum of their growth, however, is somewhat disturbing, and the extensive involvement of private creditors reinforces that concern. The danger is that soaring debt service obligations might force a number of countries into payments difficulties which could conceivably spread on a large scale.

In view of this precarious situation, surgery is sometimes contemplated in the form of a general debt relief operation. Such a course of action is neither advisable nor necessary.

As a policy, it would create a fair amount of confusion. The magnitudes involved are of the same order as those in the oil crisis. It is unlikely that developed countries would be willing and able to mobilize the vast amounts of public funds required. This view, however, should not apply to commercial countries in the same way as to aid-dependent countries. For the latter, external financing largely remains an official, development assistance-related undertaking. The case for an official rearrangement of their debts can accordingly be a practical one. For commercial countries, on the contrary, rearrangements could prove disruptive because of the commercial nature of the debt relationship. Indeed, as extensive diplomatic evaluation and a number of test cases have shown in recent years, this is not considered a practical option by borrowers themselves.

Another course of action would be to maintain a high growth rate of disbursements, so that new loans keep running ahead of debt service payments. In view of the current levels of indebtedness, this policy is too hazardous. Further additions to the level of debt, relative to exports, would strongly increase the probability of extensive roll-over difficulties. Unplanned cuts in the net resource transfer in the face of rising debt service obligations would oblige a number of developing countries to restrict their imports, at a high cost to themselves in terms of foregone domestic growth, but also to industrial nations in terms of foregone exports. Altogether, the growth of world trade would be seriously impaired. The loss of foreign exchange earnings for middle-income countries in that case far outweighs the gains that can be achieved from pushing the growth of debt to any sensibly sustainable ceiling. It does not pay to take that chance.

Therefore the sensible policy is to cut down the growth of disbursements. This will lessen the risks of disruptions of debt service and of world trade; it will also squeeze out the net transfer, as debt service catches up with new loans. Continued adjustment on the part of commercial developing countries is necessary to accommodate this plan, but they alone cannot manage. A sustained growth of world trade, fueled by import demand in industrial countries, is required to provide developing countries with the foreign exchange for their development and with an expanding base in support of their external liabilities. The traps in the way of trade expansion are clear; it must be realized that time to overcome them is running short. Official lending must also be resumed to improve roll-over conditions for commercial countries and above all for the benefit of aid-dependent countries, for which continued assistance remains absolutely crucial.

Unless a recovery prevails in industrial countries, exports of developing regions will not increase sufficiently, crises will become more frequent, and their repetition may turn sluggishness into a recession. Depression is still around the corner. It can be avoided, but not unless the contributing forces are properly evaluated.

Part I
A New Debt

A survey of recent debt developments is useful to identify the major trends of the last few years. The more obvious of these trends is the strong increase in debt activity, that is, in the level of debt outstanding and in the size of debt flows. A development less obvious, but of equal import, is the growing share of debt activity accounted for by private lenders and the middle-income borrowing countries. The most substantive development is the combination of these two trends. The upsurge in debt activity is more than a temporary phenomenon, because it is supported by changes in market structure. While the strong growth of debt may be the more striking fact, the more significant one is the momentum of that growth.

These points are investigated here on the basis of the public debt of developing countries, as covered under the World Bank's "Debtor Reporting System." The coverage includes external medium- and long-term foreign currency debts which are a direct liability or are guaranteed by public bodies in the borrowing countries. For practical purposes, the data are available in the Bank's "World Trade Tables," an annual mimeographed publication, and in summary form in its annual reports. The latest available data, published in 1978, cover the debt status of ninety-six countries, including nine oil exporters, as of the end of 1976. Earlier editions covered a smaller number of reporting countries, for example, eighty-four countries in the 1977 edition. The "World Debt Tables" is the standard source used here. Throughout this book all references are made to public debt, so that mentions of private or official loans are intended to designate loans from private or official creditors involving the public sector of the borrowing countries.

1 To the Hilt: The Change in Total Debt

A powerful surge of new loans resulting in a steep accumulation of outstanding liabilities has pushed the external debt of developing countries from $75 billion in 1970 to $227 billion at the end of 1976 (table 1-1). Moreover, nominal lending conditions have become harder, because of increased contributions of private lenders acting on market terms. As a consequence the growth of external debts will not subside shortly: as loans have expanded in the past, so debt service is expanding now. New loans must therefore be arranged in enlarged amounts to refinance the old ones, and so on.

"To the hilt," exclaims Governor Angelopoulos.[1] Yet, the increase in borrowers' exports has also been impressive, so that the size of debt, relative to exports, has not changed very much. Rather than the level of debt, the momentum of its growth is a source of concern.

Overall Trends

Loan disbursements to ninety-six developing countries were over three times as large in 1976 as in 1971; allowing for debt service payments, the net transfer of resources was over four times as large. Debt outstanding meanwhile had increased 2½ times.

The increase has not been even over the period. The steepest growth (figure 1-1) was recorded during 1975, when the recession in industrial countries created the context for very large current account deficits of the developing countries. Disbursements in that year increased by 36 percent over their 1974 level, and the net transfer soared by 68 percent. This was really the boom year, flaring off a new round of concern, talk, and negotiations about the debt problems of developing countries. By and large, however, it was only the extreme point of an acceleration which was initiated at the turn of the present decade.

Historical data on external debt are somewhat sketchy. Estimates compiled by the World Bank indicate that the debt outstanding of seventy-one countries, including undisbursed amounts, was multiplied by somewhat over four between 1955 and 1965.[2] For more recent years, table 1-1 shows that its growth abated to 12 percent per year from 1965 to 1969, trebled in ten years, and accelerated strongly from 1971, to the rate of a sixfold increase in ten years.

Table 1-1
Developing Countries: External Public Debt, 1965-1977
(billions of U.S. dollars)

	Outstanding Including Undisbursed (End of Year)	*Disbursements*	*Debt Service*	*Net Transfer*
1965[a]	37.5	6.1	3.4	2.7
1966	42.7	5.9	3.8	2.1
1967	48.4	7.4	4.0	3.4
1968	54.3	8.1	4.5	3.6
1969	59.3	8.2	5.0	3.2
1970	75.1	11.1	6.2	4.9
1971	88.7	12.3	7.0	5.3
1972	103.2	15.5	8.7	6.8
1973	125.0	21.3	11.7	9.6
1974	157.2	25.5	14.2	11.3
1975	186.3	34.7	15.7	19.0
1976	227.4	40.2	18.2	22.0
1977[b]	272.5	56.9	28.7	28.2

Source: Based on World Bank, *Annual Reports,* 1971, appendix tables 5 and 9, and 1978, appendix tables 4 and 8.

[a]Eighty countries for 1965 to 1969; ninety-six countries thereafter.

[b]Preliminary estimates based on World Bank, "World Debt Tables," mimeographed, Washington, 1978.

Recent growth can therefore be considered much larger than in previous experience. Historical performance—doubling every five years from $89 billion in 1971—would have resulted in a debt of about $178 billion in 1976. The "excess" is therefore about $50 billion, which is not so much—barely 1.2 percent of the gross annual output of Organization for Economic Cooperation and Development (OECD) countries—but which is also a lot: 20 percent of annual investment in developing countries, or two-thirds of the cumulative current account surplus of Kuwait, Libya, and Saudi Arabia from 1974 to 1976.

In spite of its acceleration, however, the growth of debt outstanding has not outpaced that of exports. In fact, the aggregate debt ratio for eighty-four countries, that is to say total debt outstanding disbursed divided by total merchandise exports, declined from 115 percent in 1972 to 84 percent in 1976. Excluding oil exporters, which have, of course, benefited from a peculiarly strong increase in exports, these results still hold: the external debt of nonoil developing countries was smaller relative to exports in 1976 (112 percent) than in 1972 (125 percent).

The explanation, of course, lies in the very strong inflation of the period; unit export values for nonoil developing countries have more than doubled from 1971 to 1976. This trend benefited all regions, although it was stronger in some, as in Latin America, than in others, as in South Asia.

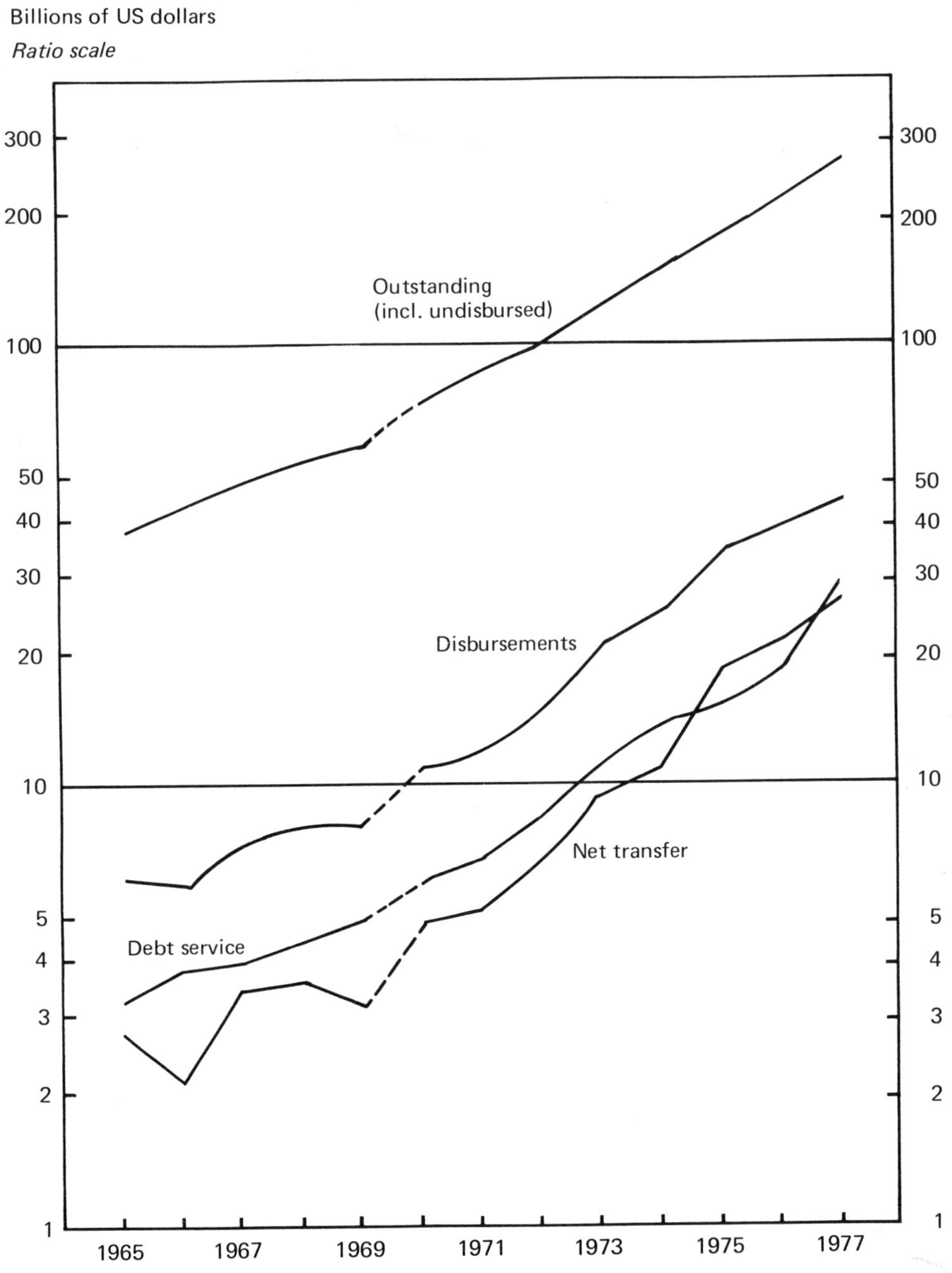

Source: Table 1-1.

Figure 1-1. Developing Countries: External Public Debt.

In real terms, therefore, the growth of debt was much smaller than nominal figures would suggest; indeed, in real terms, it decelerated in recent years. By using the industrial countries' unit export value index to measure the purchasing power of debt, the growth of real debt falls from 14 percent per year from 1965 to 1971 to 7 percent from 1971 to 1976: the drop is sharp enough to dwarf the uncertainties in the figures.

Inflation also mitigated the impact of harder terms. While the nominal interest rate on loans to developing countries has been rising throughout the period, it has been historically low in real terms. In recent years, debt has accumulated on negative real interest rates. As indicated on table 1-2, prevailing real rates were 3 to 4 percent in the 1960s. They became consistently negative in the 1970s, except for a brief spell in 1976, because nominal rates, while rising, did not keep up with the surge in export prices of industrial countries. This, of course, contributed massively to the achievement of the real transfer of resources during the period. Negative interest rates, however, can only be transitory phenomena, and the return to positive real rates will impose stringent constraints on debt management.

Creditor Structure and the Surge of Debt Service

The large nominal growth rate of debt in recent years is more than a temporary disturbance, because it has been accompanied by a major structural change in the composition of capital flows.

First, debt accumulation has accounted for a growing share of the resource transfer to developing countries. The International Monetary Fund's annual reports thus indicate that transactions which do not affect debt positions amounted to 80 percent of the net change in debt of developing countries other than those in South Europe in 1973. That share fell steadily to 45 percent in 1976, although it picked up to 50 percent in 1977.

Underlying that change is the stagnation of financing such as public unrequited transfers and net direct investment from 1974 to 1976. In view of inflationary conditions in these years, this is a substantive reduction in real terms. It is not a plain accident. Official development assistance (ODA) of members of the Development Assistance Committee experienced a downward trend over the last ten years: ODA was 0.44 percent of their gross domestic product in 1965 and barely 0.3 percent in 1977. This shortfall alone more than explains the acceleration in the growth of debt in recent years. Direct investment similarly has been on the decline, because investors found it wiser to trade some equity exposure for a more readily insurable debt exposure. Altogether, in spite of the relatively large flows the Organization of Petroleum-Exporting Countries, these trends were aggravated from 1974 to 1976: grants and direct investment financed 57 per-

Table 1-2
Interest Rate on Loan Commitments to Developing Countries, 1965-1976
(percent)

	Nominal Rate[a]	*Price Deflator*[b]	*Real Rate*[c]
1965	4.3	2.2	2.1
1966	4.0	2.2	1.8
1967	4.6	–	4.6
1968	4.8	–	4.8
1969	5.2	2.1	3.1
1970	5.3	6.1	–0.8
1971	5.6	5.8	–0.2
1972	5.6	9.1	–3.3
1973	6.2	20.0	–13.0
1974	6.4	23.6	–16.1
1975	6.6	12.3	–5.3
1976	6.8	–	6.8

Sources: World Bank, *Annual Reports*, 1971, appendix table 10, and 1978, appendix table 9; and International Monetary Fund, *International Financial Statistics*, May 1978.

[a]Average rate on new commitments to developing countries; based on eighty countries for 1965 to 1969 and on ninety-six countries for 1970 to 1976.

[b]Change in the U.S. dollar unit value index for exports of industrial countries.

[c]Ratio of the above rates.

cent of the nonoil countries' current account deficit over the three years (1971 to 1973) prior to the oil shock and covered only 35 percent of that deficit over the next three years.[3]

The vacuum thus created was filled with rising debt flows, but under new conditions.

A salient feature of the changing debt structure is a larger share of private financing. As shown in table B-1, the debt of developing countries to private creditors increased markedly faster from 1972 to 1975 than their liabilities to official creditors: the former more than doubled, while the latter increased by only 60 percent. The share of official commitments in total lending, which was 55 to 60 percent until 1972, dropped to 46 percent in 1975. While still the largest, with over 60 percent of total outstanding, the share of official lending has thus clearly declined, a trend which carried into 1976 and 1977.

Significantly, however, the net transfer from official loans accounted for a sustained share—about half—of the total in 1975 as well as in 1972. This is a reflection of the rapid increase in debt service on private loans, owing to their nonconcessional terms: debt service increased by 58 percent for official loans in three years to 1975, as against 87 percent for private loans and 125 percent for loans from private financial markets.

The period also witnessed extensive changes in the structure of official as well as private lending.

Multilateral institutions have increased their share of official commitments at the expense of bilateral flows. In fact, multilateral institutions, of which the World Bank is the largest by far, have maintained their share of total commitments as well as of net transfer and debt outstanding.

The relative decline in official lending therefore entirely reflects the trends of bilateral lending, which compounds the fall in unrequited transfers. Their decline would show even more sharply were it not for the swift increase in commitments of OPEC countries: already in 1975, new commitments by these countries reached $4.6 billion as against $7.2 billion for governments of the Development Assistance Committee, which had fallen by then to 16 percent of total official and private commitments.

The salient fact about private loans is the rising relative importance of financial markets, including the banks and bond markets, which accounted for over 40 percent of total commitments in 1975. The direct role of bond markets has only become significant in 1977; until then, their contribution was mostly confined to the refinancing of multilateral institutions. Banks, however, have been directly involved since the turn of the decade. In all respects, they have been the most rapidly growing source of external funds to developing countries over the period, while officially insured suppliers' credits relinquished their formerly dominant position.

One favorable consequence of these developments has been the facilitation of the management of external loans: the paperwork involved in bank lending, where bulk transactions are standard, is less, and more importantly these resources are not tied to project or procurement conditions as suppliers credits are.

On the other hand, the relative decline in official bilateral lending and the step-up in bank financing have resulted in harder terms. Also the grant element of commitments to ninety-six developing countries, which is a synthetic measure of the "softness" of the loans, fell from 27 percent in 1972 to 18 percent in 1976. The new structure of commitments explains much of this deterioration, although the terms for each category of loans also became harder (table B-2). Additional deterioration resulted from the relative decline in grants, and the grant element of loans and grants combined was cut by one-third in four years, dropping to 22 percent in 1976.

The full impact of harder terms will bear in 1979 and beyond, at the very moment when disbursements might well slow down: debt service is getting behind, *but* it will catch up.

That lag and its inescapable unwinding are already notarized in the debt service schedules. These schedules are not a debt service forecast, but the plain projection of debt service flows based on committed debt only. Nonetheless, they comprise a significant fraction of actual service payments.

In contrast to actual payments, scheduled charges have been growing more rapidly than outstanding debt (table 1-3). Debt service scheduled over six years was 56 percent of debt outstanding at the end of 1969, up to 68 percent at the end of 1976. Scheduled debt service will either exert a pressure to keep a high growth of disbursements to refinance it or squeeze out the net transfer. This is largely a consequence of the growing share of bank loans, which are rather "volatile." Debt service on these in a given year is typically equal to 17 percent of loans outstanding at the end of the previous year, as against 6.5 percent for official loans.[4]

This point deserves strong emphasis because it is basic to the dynamics of the system. The rise in debt service payments is inescapable; therefore so is the rise of borrowing requirements. Scheduled service payments over six years on account of 1976 outstanding debt alone were over twice as large as total actual payments over the six previous years and were equal to total disbursements over those six years. The increase in debt, and especially that of disbursements, is just a beginning. Until now, exports have globally kept in line. Will they continue to do so in the coming days where annual disbursements top $100 billion?

Such is the paradox of debt over that period: it is not so high, but it is running too fast. Its growth rate, rather than its level, is a cause for concern.

Table 1-3
Debt-Service Schedules, 1969, 1972, 1976
(billions of U.S. dollars and percent)

	1969[a]	*1972*[b]	*1976*[c]
Cumulative payments scheduled: over following six years:			
In billion dollars			
On total debt	33.4	61.0	155.2
On debt to banks	3.6	11.5	64.1
As percentage of debt outstanding, including undisbursed:			
On total debt	56.2	61.3	68.4
On debt to banks	99.7	105.5	108.1

Source: Computed from World Bank, *Annual Reports* 1971 appendix table 8, 1974 appendix table 7, and 1978, appendix table 7.

[a]Eighty countries.

[b]Eighty-six countries.

[c]Ninety-six countries.

2 Commercial Borrowers and Aid-Dependent Countries

As there are vast differences between the various sources of capital to developing countries, there are also wide differences among borrowers. Some are well advanced on the road to development and have the capacity to borrow on commercial terms; others have not yet reached a stage of self-supporting growth and require foreign capital on aid terms to assist them in their takeoff.

The distinction between "commercial" and "aid-dependent" developing countries has become sharper in recent years; it has also commanded more attention. It is based on the economic performance of countries in the "middle-income" range. These countries have a large economic potential and have managed a very high average rate of economic growth since 1960—twice as large as that of the low-income countries and about one-half larger than in industrial countries. In many respects, their economic structure is now comparable to that of the developed countries, while income and structural change in low-income countries was much less extensive.

This trend has been reinforced in the mid-1970s as the economic difficulties of industrial countries contrasted with the unabating growth of middle-income regions. On that occasion, the implications of this trend for the status of external debts and the allocation of foreign capital became ominous.

Middle-income countries have absorbed the bulk of private loans in recent years, notably those from private banks, which comprised most of the increase in net flows. This policy helped them sustain their high growth rate, but it was also instrumental in facilitating the recycling of oil surpluses. The private origin of the loans and their contribution to international adjustment both indicate that the debt of middle-income countries has assumed a commercial character which contrasts with the developmental, official relationship of previous experience and with the continuing experience of low-income countries.

Growth Performance

Table 2-1 presents selected data on the comparative status of low-income countries, including Indonesia, and of middle-income countries, including other capital-deficit oil exporters.

Table 2-1
Developing Countries: Growth Performance 1960-1975

Grouping[a]	*Low Income*	*Middle Income*	*All Developing*	*Industrial*
Population 1975 (billions)	1.2	0.9	2.1	0.7
GDP, 1975 ($ billion)	180	869	1,049	3,841
Exports 1976 ($ billion)	21	188	209	636
Real GDP growth (percent per year)				
1960-1970	2.8[b]	6.3	5.5	4.9
1970-1975	3.8[b]	6.4	5.9	2.8
Share of investment in GDP (percent)				
1960	14.7	20.2	19.9	21.9
1965	19.1	26.4	24.6	20.6

Sources: World Bank, *World Development Report,* Washington, 1978, chap. 2, and *Annual Report,* appendix table 1

[a]Low-income countries are those with a per capita income of up to $250 in 1976. This category includes Indonesia. Middle-income countries include those in Southern Europe and capital-deficit oil exporters other than Indonesia. Industrialized countries are those in the OECD area except Greece, Portugal Spain and Turkey. Centrally planned economies and countries with populations of less than 1 million are not covered in this table.

[b]Author's estimates.

Some 1,200 million people are living in the thirty-four low-income countries with a population of over 1 million. Their combined output of $180 billion is only 4 percent of world production; their exports, of $21 billion represent a still lower 2.5 percent share, of which India and Indonesia alone account for the greatest part ($14 billion). These countries are still registering average investment ratios well below those in the other groups, and their cumulative growth over the last fifteen years has barely reached 60 percent.[1]

The low-income countries are mostly located in Africa, south of the Sahara, and South Asia, with most of the population and economic potential located in the latter region. Low-income Africa is indeed faced with particularly severe difficulties. Its growth rate fell from an average annual 4.3 percent in the 1960s to 2.8 percent from 1970 to 1975, and its savings ratio is still a meager 8.4 percent, contributing to less than half of the investments realized in the region. Low-income Asia, on the other hand, has managed to increase its growth rate from 2.4 percent in the 1960s to 3.9 percent from 1970 to 1975, and its savings ratio of 16.7 percent is financing over 85 percent of investment in the region.

For all their diversity, these regions have the common feature of being home to some 600 million absolute poor. Prospects for even a modest reduction in that appalling number are predicated not only on improved savings and investment policies, but also on a continuing inflow of external aid. Aid, not commercial lending, is a necessity in their case. It is also a feasible solution. As is well known, the official development assistance extended by developed countries, at 0.36 percent of GNP in 1975, falls halfway short of the United Nations' target of 0.7 percent. The shortfall of $13.5 billion is equivalent to 39 percent of investment in low-income countries in 1975. In other words, meeting the United Nations' target would be enough to raise the investment ratio in these countries by 7 points to a comfortable 26 percent—which is not a sufficient condition for development, but at least removes a major obstacle.

The fifty-eight countries with a per capita income in excess of $250 and populations of over 1 million comprise fewer inhabitants (0.9 billion) than low-income regions, but their $870 billion gross product is nearly five times as large, and their $188 billion exports are nine times as large. The sheer economic magnitudes involved are very different; to use the above yardstick, the shortfall in ODA is barely equivalent to a 1.5 percent increase in the investment ratio of middle-income countries, which is already in excess of 26 percent.

With a combined GNP amounting to 23 percent of that of industrial countries, the middle-income countries not only carry substantial economic weight, but are also performing very strongly: their GNP has increased by 150 percent in real terms since 1960, as against 85 percent for industrial countries. This strong performance is likely to continue because it has been matched by extensive structural change and has become largely self-supporting. The investment ratio in middle-income countries has been up to the standards of developed countries for a number of years, and in recent years this has also been true of the savings ratio. A continued inflow of foreign resources is no longer essential to the growth performance of these countries as a whole, although it may still be in some individual cases. In addition, a sizable manufacturing sector has been developed. Industry has been the fastest-growing sector in these economies, and its median share in total output has increased from 20 to 32 percent in 1976, as compared with 41 percent in industrial countries. The share of manufactures in total exports, while still a modest figure globally, has trebled in fifteen years (1960 to 1975). Indeed, it has become dominant or large for a number of countries: South Korea (14 percent of exports in 1960, 82 percent in 1975), Jamaica (5 and 55 percent), Brazil (3 and 27 percent), Mexico (12 and 53 percent), and the countries in South Europe among them. Manufactures have largely contributed to the growth of nonfuel export earnings. The nonoil countries which experienced export growth in excess of 15 percent per year include notably Korea, Spain, Israel, Lebanon, Malta, Portugal, and Taiwan (for all of which exports of manufactures are in excess of half of total exports), as well as Brazil, Greece, Costa Rica, and Singapore (for which that share ranges between 20 and 50 percent).

Included in the group of middle-income countries are the capital-deficit oil exporters other than Indonesia, a low-income country. These countries have taken advantage of the oil price increase in the form of a sharp boost in their export earnings, which amount to about $70 billion, or over 35 percent of the total for middle-income countries. However, they have displayed an ability to absorb an equally large increase in imports and have resumed their external borrowing. Indeed, from 1972 to 1976 oil producers have not displayed lesser reliance on debt than nonoil countries (table B-3). This, and the discovery of large (for example, in Mexico) or small (for example, in Cameroon) oil deposits in a number of other countries, has reduced the significance of the "oil country" status.

Two other outstanding groups among middle-income countries are those in Southern Europe—Spain, Greece, Turkey, Portugal, and Yugoslavia—which for many purposes could be considered developed (and indeed are so classified by a number of international organizations)—and those in Latin America. The latter include such large countries as Brazil with a 1976 GDP of $127 billion, Argentina ($93 billion), and Mexico ($75 billion), which together account for nearly 30 percent of the combined GNP of all middle-income countries, a fact with obvious relevance for the distribution of external debt.

Contrary to the case of industrial countries, the growth performance of the middle-income countries has been relatively unaffected by the economic difficulties of the mid-1970s. Their real growth rate increased rather marginally over the record of the 1960s, a result which owes more to policies in nonoil countries than to the growth of oil producers. Because of this, the gap between middle-income and industrial countries was further reduced. At the same time, there was a strong increase in nonoil trade between these two groups, as well as increased recognition that further trade expansion, not aid, has become the key issue in their relations.

Access to Financial Markets

The differences in income levels and growth rates among the low- and middle-income developing countries are reflected in their access to the various sources of external financing.

The access of a given country to external financial sources is a complex phenomenon. Foreign capital is not a homogeneous good, but comprises a spectrum of instruments which can be diversely substituted for one another. Demand and supply originate from various sources, and each particular flow interacts with all others. The supply of Eurocurrency credits to Korea, for example, depends on its borrowing requirements, on its ability to accept given terms, on what it can obtain from official creditors, and on the alternative lending opportunities creditors can find in other countries. In addition, as is seen later, a number of "extraneous" factors are operative. Altogether, there is little scope for being able to foretell precisely how much a country can expect to be able to borrow on what terms.

There is, however, a possibility of developing substantive guidelines in this respect. As evidenced from aggregate data, the allocation of foreign capital is not indeterminate, but falls into a definite pattern. In order to get a clearer determination of that pattern, a more specific identification of the problem is required as well as additional data.

The concept of access to external finance is essentially a relative one. A country is not "good" for so many millions—it is "good" for such a share of the pie, whether that pie is the investment portfolio of a commercial bank or the budget constraint of a government aid agency. Not all lenders have the same perception of what is an adequate distribution of their portfolio.

The following evidence from aggregate data suggests that a broad dividing line runs between official and private lenders. The dividing line, of course, is not clear-cut; such entities as export credit agencies, for example, may be hard to classify. There are also substantial differences within each category, for example, between official concessional (development assistance) loans and official loans on market terms. Nevertheless, the distribution of private loans, as opposed to public ones, can be expected to reflect market principles, while public institutions would emphasize development needs. Indeed, the latter assignment has been partly institutionalized. Access to the resources of the International Development Agency, for example, is restricted to countries in the low-income or lower middle-income ranges. Likewise, following the oil crisis, select "most seriously affected," "landlocked," "island," or "Sahel" country groups have been singled out for special attention.

Relevant considerations in exercising these preferences relate to the borrower's needs and capacity to borrow. The latter is relevant to determine risk, and under market principles the perception of risk will guide the distribution of the investment portfolio. Borrowing capacity is not a unique figure, however; it depends notably on the terms of the loans. Accordingly, risk evaluation is also relevant for official lenders who should step in where borrowing capacity under market terms is insufficient to meet the objectives of development.

Finally, the variables which are relevant to guide the behavior of lenders should also be relevant for borrowers. These also need to weigh "need" against "capacity to borrow," because overborrowing is not any more sensible than overlending. Actually, in a number of statistical experiments, it was not possible to devise concepts which would be specific to lenders or to borrowers. This means that in the observation of the country distribution of loans, the supply could not be distinguished from the demand. However, as detailed later, it is believed that a rationing system is operative, so that the observed distribution is really a representation of the supply of loans. Rationing is a logical assumption in the case of official loans which, because they are cheap, must, by definition, be in short supply. In the case of private loans the assumption is more controversial: potential rationing will exist, in the form of exposure limits, but not all borrowers will borrow up to the limit.

These expectations are borne out by evidence drawn from the distribution of external loans to thirty-one countries in the 1969-1971 average. That distribution (see appendix C) has been examined jointly in respect of the volume and of the terms of official and private loans.

Regarding the volume of official loans relative to the borrowers' exports, the sample evidence indicates that poorer countries and/or those with a higher debt service ratio receive relatively larger official commitments.

The consideration of income per capita in that connection is a straightforward indication of the aid function of official lending. The role of the debt service ratio probably reflects the need to achieve a larger inflow of fresh money in those countries where the debt service is higher, in order to obtain a given resource transfer. That explanation would be consistent with the fact that debt service ratios also positively influence the allocation of private loans: larger gross loans can be extended for a given exposure when repayments are larger. In both cases, a dynamic reformulation, treating debt as an "endogenous" variable, would be worthwhile. In the present static framework, however, there is no doubt that debt service influences the flow of commitments, not the reverse; and the same holds for the role of GNP.

The terms of official loans, measured through their grant element, are adjustable. While each particular institution enjoys only limited flexibility in this respect, cofinancing among diverse sources, whether formally arranged or not, provides a measure of adaptability. Terms of official lending are thus found to be more concessional for those countries with a low income per capita and/or a low GNP growth rate.

The sensitivity of official terms to the GNP growth rate is noteworthy. A slow-growing country can absorb a greater amount of external loans only if the terms are softer. Otherwise debt service will rapidly eat up the better part of the newly borrowed foreign exchange. It is therefore consistent that the slower-growing countries, being also the poorer ones, should benefit from softer terms: they need them to absorb a larger volume of assistance.

The flexibility of official terms does not mean that they are negotiable. The sample evidence indicates that loan volume and loan terms are not related, in the sense that you cannot trade some soft loans for a larger amount of harder ones. Rather, both terms and volume seem to result from lenders' perception of need, suggesting that official loans are basically rationed out.

Rationing also seems to be relevant, albeit along different procedures, in the case of private loans.

Sample evidence in respect to these loans indicates that (1) countries with a higher GNP growth rate and/or a higher debt service ratio can obtain a larger volume of private commitments, and (2) all countries get essentially the same loan terms.

Here again, borrowers appear to be in the position of price takers: they cannot induce lenders into accepting a greater exposure by offering harder terms. Of course, some differentiation of terms is possible through the mechanism of "spreads." Nevertheless, there is only limited flexibility in this respect. This is explained by Kapur[2] as profit-maximizing behavior on the part of lenders: raising the rate of interest on a loan to a marginal borrower also increases the probability of default on that loan, so that the expected net return is not improved. Accordingly, there is little scope for terms adjustment, and available resources are allocated on the basis of perceived relative capacities to borrow, which, under set terms, depend on relative economic performance.

To sum up, the evidence from cross-sectional data reveals an adjustment of the supply of external loans to the recipients' capacity to borrow. That capacity is determined jointly by the terms of the loans and the borrowers' economic performance; and adjustment of the terms of official loans and of the volume of private loans tends to match the borrowers' exposure and their capacity. In so doing, however, the market also allows for a number of other considerations.

One of the more systematic "extraneous" considerations involved is the borrower's "size" in absolute economic terms: small countries tend to obtain relatively more loans than large ones. This "small-country bias" has been evidenced by deVries, who found that in each of several per capita income ranges small countries receive more loans than large ones, and these loans have a larger grant element.[3] Further, the small-country bias appears to hold whatever the income range and to be so pronounced as to dominate the per capita income effect. Small countries in the highest income range receive more aid as a percentage of GNP than large countries in the lowest income range.

The small-country bias is largely a noneconomic factor, whose role has been reinforced indirectly by the consideration given to special geographic features; most of the "seriously affected," "island," or "landlocked" countries are small in terms of population or GNP. This bias is probably fairly instrumental in explaining the large relative amounts of external assistance received by low-income countries in Africa, as compared to those in South Asia. However, deVries indicates that this bias may have an economic rationale, because the small size of a country would be a handicap to economic growth, being an obstacle to diversified industrial investment and to the development of a broad financial system, or again because of relatively larger "overhead" costs of maintaining a governmental structure.

Another "extraneous" consideration of a different nature is the existence of a consortium or consultative group backing up the borrowing country. Aid coordination groups have been established, most under International Bank for Reconstruction and Development (IBRD) auspices, for eighteen countries. In three cases (India, Turkey, and Pakistan) they have been established in the form of consortia, meaning that developed-country members are pledging specific assistance. In other cases, no such pledge is taken, but the existence of the group provides an assurance of goodwill and mutual confidence.

Based on the evidence of the sample of thirty-one countries, it would appear that the existence of a consultative group does result in a larger volume of official loans to the relevant country, but has no bearing on the terms of the loans or on access to private financing. The influence of consultative groups on the volume of aid is additional to the influence of the relatively low average income per capita of consultative group countries. Just as the small-country bias does, it reinforces the preferential assignment of official loans to the poorer countries.

The Structure of International Lending

As a result of lenders' policies and of the diverse economic performances of borrowers, there are substantive differences in the creditor composition of the debts of low- and middle-income countries. As pointed out by Beim,[5] low-income countries are aid-dependent in that they cannot absorb substantial amounts of foreign loans at market terms, but require long-term, low-interest loans from nonmarket sources. Middle-income countries, on the other hand, can draw on commercial bank financing and have absorbed the bulk of private loans in recent years.

Statistical evidence of this situation obtains from the creditor composition of debt outstanding. As shown in table 2-2, low-income countries are overwhelmingly indebted to official creditors, the debt of middle-income countries is evenly distributed between private and official lenders, and private creditors hardly lend anything to low income-countries (whatever small amounts are recorded are mostly on account of Zaire and Indonesia, two "special cases" in which the banks wish they had not stepped in).

Using a broader concept of external resources, including grants and direct investment, leads to similar conclusions. As shown in table 2-3, net private flows to low-income countries were less than 9 percent of total private flows in the 1973-1976 average and accounted for only 18 percent of total net flows to these countries, while they provided middle-income countries with a full 60 percent of external resources during that period.

Table 2-2
Ninety-six Developing Countries: Creditor Distribution of Debt Outstanding (Disbursed) by Income Class, 1972 and 1976
(billions of U.S. dollars, end of period[a])

Country Group	1972 Official Creditors	1972 Private Creditors	1972 Total	1976 Official Creditors	1976 Private Creditors	1976 Total
Low-income	21.5	3.0	24.5	38.4	7.9	46.3
Middle-income	27.4	22.3	49.7	49.4	64.8	114.2
Total	48.9	25.3	74.2	87.9	72.7	160.5

Source: IBRD, "World Debt Tables," mimeographed, Washington, 1978.

[a]Details may not add to totals because of rounding. Low-income countries are those with a 1976 per capita income of $280 or less.

Tables 2-2 and 2-3 indicate a few further points. Low-income countries account for about one-quarter of the total external debt of developing countries, as against 10 percent of their exports. Their debt is therefore relatively heavier, a fact that can be partly explained by the high sensitivity of debt outstanding to the maturity of the loans, which is longer for the official loans. In addition, the net flow of loan resources to low-income countries from 1972 to 1975 has been very sizable, compared to their GNP. Still, because of their sheer size, middle-income countries absorbed over 75 percent of the total net flow of the period, and still hold 60 percent of liabilities to official creditors.

Table 2-3
Creditor Distribution of the Net Flow of External Resources by Income Class, 1973-1975 Average[a]
(billions of U.S. dollars)

	Low-Income Countries	Middle-Income Countries	Total
Official development assistance	6.4	6.9	13.3
Other official flows	0.4	3.5	3.9
Private flows	1.5	15.6	17.1
Direct investments	(0.9)	(8.1)	(9.0)
Exports credits	(0.3)	(1.5)	(1.8)
Eurocurrency credits	(0.3)	(6.0)	(6.3)
Total	8.3	26.0	34.3

Source: Computed from "Development Co-operation–Efforts and Policies of the Members of the Development Assistance Committee" (Paris: OECD, 1977), table III-2.

[a]The coverage and country classification in this table differ slightly from those in table 2-2.

Because of regional differences in income levels, the debt status of developing countries also varies depending on geographic location.

Latin America stands out as "the" debtor region, with over 30 percent of total debt outstanding, nearly half of the liabilities to private banks, and over 40 percent of total disbursements and debt service payments in 1976. Since these amounts are concentrated on a small number of countries, developments in that region are of particular importance (tables 2-4 and 2-5).

More generally, two broad area groupings can be identified. The first comprises the middle-income countries in Latin America, Southern Europe, and East Asia. They rely on commercial financing, but their debt-to-GNP ratio is not the higher of the two. On the other hand, the low-income regions in Africa, the Middle East, and South Asia have large debt-to-GNP ratios, but have accumulated their debts on rather favorable terms, allowing for better roll-over conditions. Debt service in South Asia absorbed only 41 percent of new loans in 1975 as against 47 percent for Latin America. Debt service amounted to 4 percent of debt outstanding, including undisbursed, in the former region and to 11 percent in the latter. The problems of debt management are rather different in the low- and the middle-income regions: middle-income regions must roll over each year a much larger share of their debts, and this is mainly because of their creditor structure.

The matching of private creditors with "commercial" borrowers thus also bears on the distribution of debt service, a significant point for the definition of guidelines for multilateral debt renegotiations. A one-year moratorium in Latin America would "freeze" 9 percent of the banks' claims on developing countries; the same in Africa would freeze only 0.6 percent of official claims. In this respect, too, Latin America is "the" debtor region.

Table 2-4
Ninety-six Developing Countries: Regional Distribution of External Debt, 1976[a]
(billions of U.S. dollars)

	Debt Outstanding Including Undisbursed			
	Total	*Of Which Due to Banks*	*Disbursements*	*Debt Service*
Africa south of the Sahara	24.5	4.2	3.6	1.4
South Asia	30.5	0.2	3.1	1.3
North Africa and the Middle East	37.5	8.9	6.2	2.9
Latin America	68.5	28.4	16.2	7.6
East Asia	38.7	10.3	6.6	2.8
Southern Europe	27.8	7.3	4.4	2.2
Total of all countries	227.4	59.3	40.2	18.2

Source: World Bank, *Annual Report*, 1978, appendix tables 4 and 8.
[a]Items may not add to totals because of rounding.

Table 2-5
Ninety-six Developing Countries: Regional Distribution of Debt-Service Indicators, 1976
(percent)

	Debt Service as Percentage of Disbursements, 1976	*Cumulative Scheduled Debt Service 1977-1980, as Percentage of Outstanding, Including Undisbursed, End of 1976*	*Grant Element of New Commitments 1976*
Africa south of the Sahara	38.7	37.5	31 0
South Asia	40.7	21.6	52.0
North Africa and the Middle East	46 3	45.5	20.0
Latin America	47.1	66.4	11.0
East Asia	42.3	46.6	12.0
Southern Europe	50.6	53.1	17.0
Total of all countries	45.3	48.8	18.0

Source: Based on World Bank *Annual Report,* 1978, appendix tables 7, 8, and 9

The Heavyweights

While it reveals a wide diversity of situations, the classification of borrowers by income level and geographic location does not sufficiently evidence the extent to which external debt is concentrated over a few countries.

At the end of 1975, there were eight countries with debts, including undisbursed, in excess of $6 billion each: Algeria, Brazil, India, Indonesia, Iran, Korea, Mexico, and Pakistan, with total debts of $84 billion, that is, nearly half of the total for eighty-four countries. The concentration was even greater for bank loans, with four countries (Algeria, Brazil, Indonesia, and Mexico), each with an exposure of over $2.5 billion, holding half of the liabilities to the financial markets. Allowing also for Egypt and Turkey, which have heavy official debts, and Argentina, a large "private" borrower, this makes up a group of eleven countries which held 54 percent of the debt to official creditors and 60 percent of that to private ones. They secured 47 percent of official commitments in 1975 and 65 percent of private commitments.

Matching their large debts, these countries also ran impressive GNPs: $472 billion in the aggregate, which is over half of the total for the eighty-four surveyed countries. Three of them (Brazil, Mexico and India) registered together a $265 billion GNP and $42 billion in debts, amounting, respectively, to 29 and 24 percent of the total for the eighty-four countries.

While being all "heavyweights," these countries are very diverse. They can be arranged in two broad groups. Indonesia, India, Egypt, and Pakistan have a low income per capita and rely mostly on official capital.

Their debt management is under close supervision from international consortia. Indonesia is the only country in that group with significant liabilities to private creditors; these arise from consolidated trade liabilities. Egypt only recently joined the big debtor league, thanks to OPEC assistance. India's and Pakistan's debt-to-export ratios are very high; however, because of the large grant elements for their borrowings (66 and 46 percent, respectively, for the 1973-1975 average), their debt service ratios are rather low.

The second group comprises countries with a rather high level of income per capita. Korea and Turkey nevertheless managed a continued access to official loans. Algeria, Brazil, Mexico, Argentina, and Iran, on the other hand, very much depend on commercial credits. The first three pool 42 percent of the liabilities of the eighty-four countries to the financial markets and account for over half of their increase from 1972 to 1975.

Diverse but all important, these countries dominate the external financing scene of less developed countries. It is noteworthy that six of them (Argentina, Brazil, India, Indonesia, Pakistan, and Turkey) belong to the list of the eleven countries that had to stage a multilateral renegotiation of their debts between 1959 and 1976.

The relative weight of these countries is large enough to give them significant influence on changes in the debt of all countries. The wisdom of a global approach may accordingly be questioned, as compared to that of a more selective analysis.

Indeed, excluding the debt of the seven high-income heavyweights yields a new image of the situation of the seventy-seven other borrowers (table 2-6). The debt of the latter increased only by 65 percent in the three years to

Table 2-6
The Debt of Heavyweight and Other Countries, 1972 and 1975
(billions of U.S. dollars and percent)

	Seven Heavy Debtors[a]	*Seventy-seven Other Countries*	*Total of Eighty-four Countries*
Outstanding, disbursed end 1975 ($ billion)			
Total	43.2	77.8	121.0
Official creditors	17.3	54.0	71.3
Private creditors	25.9	23.8	49.7
Outstanding disbursed end 1972			
Total	21.7	47.2	68.9
Official creditors	10.2	35.8	46.0
Private creditors	11.5	11.4	22.9
Percentage increase 1972-1975			
Total	99.1	64.8	75.6
Official creditors	69.6	50.8	55.0
Private creditors	125.2	108.8	117.0

Source: World Bank, "World Debt Tables," mimeographed, Washington, 1977.
[a]Algeria, Argentina, Brazil, Iran, Korea, Mexico, Turkey.

end 1975, as compared to 100 percent for the seven heavyweights. Besides, 60 percent of net capital flows to the seventy-seven countries originated from official sources, but only one-third of those to the seven large debtors originated from official sources.

This shows the limits to general statements in the field. Yet the previously mentioned global trends cannot just be explained away as a series of individual, unrelated developments.

While scaled down to 65 percent in three years, the growth rate of debt for the seventy-seven countries remain impressive. Global conditions must have contributed to it.

Further, the structure of debt has undergone equal change in the seventy-seven countries as in the seven big debtors. Both groups have registered twice as large a growth of liabilities to private creditors as to official ones. This again points to a global influence.

Clearly, the recent trends in debt are not just the result of new capital supply arrangements. These could not have been effective save for specific policies in the debtor countries. In other words, Brazil and Mexico could have adjusted more rapidly (at what cost?) and banks' credits to developing countries would now be lesser, or more evenly distributed. To infer further that national policies are the sole underlying reason for recent debt trends would, however, be unwarranted. The point is that simultaneous adjustment of supply and demand policies has taken place under pressure from the oil shock. The global feature in recent experience is that debt became an integral part of the adjustment process.

To sum, there is evidently a set of forces operating which justify a distinction between commercial and aid-dependent countries. These forces are rather powerful, because they rest on interlocking differences between borrowers and lenders. Their combination implies that a new style of external financing has been developed, one in which the "aid" concept has lost its importance in favor of a combination of mutual interests. Accordingly, the more sensitive areas are those where this new relationship is more directly involved, that is, in bank lending to the few "heavyweights."

Part II
Overexposure?

There are limits to debt; the experience of a significant number of countries, tracing back to the nineteenth century, demonstrates the point. The identification of these limits can be challenging, because in most cases difficulties have evolved rather abruptly. Recent experience, however, is instructive; it suggests that difficulties arose from a combination of inadequate debt management and inadequate economic management. Where these pitfalls were avoided, continued reliance on external debt was possible.

The subject of debt limits has attracted renewed interest in recent years. One reason was a bold attempt by developing countries to establish new and more balanced rules for handling the debt difficulties when they arise. Another was a widespread concern that private banks might have overextended themselves in lending too much to developing countries, to the point that defaults could effectively impair their liquidity. Neither issue is yet fully settled; both have lost some of their urgency, however, because of a greater agreement that continuity in the rollover of debt outstanding is essential to both lenders and borrowers.

3 Borrowers Overexposed: The Casualties

A fair amount of resentment has been created over the past twenty years, as a number of countries, because of adverse circumstances and lax domestic policies, had to request more time for the payment of their external liabilities. As creditors proved rather unresponsive, the ensuring negotiations turned into protracted, repetitive affairs, which involved considerable foreign interference with borrowers' domestic policies.

A major attempt to change that pattern was undertaken at the Paris Conference on International Economic Cooperation, in which the debt renegotiations themselves were a topic for negotiation. The driving forces behind that attempt were of several sorts. They belonged in part to the rising self-consciousness of developing countries, but they also arose from the global context of debt accumulation in recent years. For one thing, that accumulation could be assigned to global causes, calling therefore for a general cure. For another, it involved newcomers to the debt arena—private banks—for which no established pattern of renegotiation existed.

Insofar as the attempt was made to establish a general case for debt relief, it fell over the staunch opposition of lenders in creditor countries and over the existence of conflicting interests among developing countries themselves. This is not to say, however, that the whole effort was abortive. One effective result of the undertaking was a better awareness of the specific problems of the least developed countries, resulting in some token debt forgiveness. Another was a greater awareness of the limits to possible adjustments in borrowing countries. And a third result was to achieve some measure of consensus about the crisis procedures, thus reducing the risk element in international lending and improving the access of developing countries to capital markets.

Renegotiations: The Economic Background

The experience of the twenty-odd countries which encountered major debt difficulties over the last twenty years—eleven of whom had to stage multilateral renegotiations of their debts to official creditors—is instructive for what it tells of the conditions which lead to a crisis. Those can be traced to a combination of unbalanced economic policies and inadequate debt accumulation.

Economic developments in these cases were usually characterized by heavy government spending, sometimes under inadequate control procedures, which was frequently compounded by shortfalls in export receipts.

Peru's case is illustrative in this respect. The country had to renegotiate its external debts in 1967, 1968, and then again in 1977. In both cases, the difficulty can be traced to large public sector deficits. Upon taking office in 1963, the Belaunde government endeavored to expand the economic base of the country and undertook a number of major public investment projects to this effect. Because the internal political situation would not allow for a matching increase in public revenue, the government deficit increased from 7.3 percent of revenue in 1963 to 14.1 percent in 1964 and onward to over 27 percent in 1966 and 1967. This caused domestic credit to increase rapidly, at about 20 percent per annum, although much of the government deficit was covered through foreign borrowing. While inflation was kept within reasonable bounds, this was at the cost of a deteriorating trade balance, and by 1967 an overhaul of economic policies became inevitable. This involved a devaluation of the sol, as part of a stabilization program with the International Monetary Fund (IMF), a political row with creditor governments, and a debt rescheduling in September 1968, that is, following the implementation of the stabilization program.

Ten years later, the country was in a rather similar condition for similar reasons, except that a major chunk of its debt now was owed to private banks. Heavy public spending was committed to major development projects, notably in the oil and fisheries sectors, and to military equipment. The government deficit contributed heavily to a 44 percent annual growth in domestic credit from 1974 to 1977, resulting in fairly significant inflation, and the sol was further devalued in steps from 1976. At the same time, rather than calling a formal debt conference, ongoing negotiations were held with the creditor banks. Their continued lending was made conditional on the implementation of a stabilization program, later to be supported with IMF stand-by arrangements. This mix of parallel negotiations with the banks and the IMF has been going on for about three years, and the final outcome is still uncertain.

Another case in point is that of Ghana's first renegotiation of 1966. In an effort to lessen the reliance on cocoa exports and to diversify the agriculture, Ghana undertook a large investment program, including notably the construction of the Volta River dam. The share of investment in GDP thus rose from 15 percent in 1958-1959 to 20 percent in 1963-1964. Meanwhile, prices for cocoa, the country's major export, set down to low levels before falling abruptly in 1965-1966. This, together with the long payoff period on investment projects, prevented a takeoff of domestic output, and the external current deficit on a national accounts basis was maintained at about 8 percent of GDP over the period. Further, government finances deteriorated steadily with heavy recourse to domestic bank financing; and the net external position of the banking system, which was in excess of one year's imports in 1959, turned to a net liability in 1965.

These experiences illustrate the general setting of debt crises as experienced in the past. In most cases a combination of large investment programs with deferred payoffs and deficit financing weakened the country's position. Inadequate public accounting and appropriations procedures have also been frequently involved. The most notorious case in this respect is that of Pertamina, the Indonesian oil conglomerate which managed to conduct its various operations with hardly any control from the central government—to be found burdened with a debt of over $10 billion in 1976. Export shortfalls as entailed by the drop in coffee prices prior to Brazil's 1961 renegotiation, or in copper prices prior to Chile's 1972 renegotiation, frequently added to that weakness, and because of the already rising external debt they could not be adequately offset by compensatory financing.

It is not the case, however, that all countries experiencing sustained domestic imbalances had to resort to debt renegotiations. It is the combination of such domestic developments and inadequate debt management which proved unsustainable. Conversely, high or even rising debts per se do not uniquely characterize the renegotiating countries. Rather, their distinctive feature is debt accumulated on terms inadequate to prospective growth and export performance, resulting in borrowing capacity insufficient to match actual borrowings.

Experience with past renegotiations points to such difficulties: the debt ratios of defaulting countries were rising rapidly under unfavorable terms. The two problems are linked. The borrower was accepting unfavorable terms in order to wrest a greater access to foreign capital markets; at the same time that enlarged and growing access entertained the illusion of acceptable terms, as the net resource transfer was maintained in the short run in spite of rising service payments. This could not last, and it did not.

By contrast, those countries which have not renegotiated have managed to keep the growth of their debt in line with that of their exports, accepting greater debt exposure when it was matched with improved terms.

Sustainable and Other Debts

Extensive effort has been invested in attempts to devise debt ratios and to identify the values beyond which debt difficulties could be considered likely. There is now widespread agreement that such efforts cannot substitute for a detailed analysis of the borrower's economic management and that a sort of automatic early warning is not really feasible. The tabulation of debt indicators, however, is useful, if only to obtain an idea of their usual range of variation. It can also, short of a prediction, help to understand what went wrong in the troubled cases.

A large number of indicators have been constructed. A first group expresses the relative magnitudes of debt outstanding, GNP, and exports. By convention, a high value of a debt ratio here is taken as one which is exceeded by only one-fourth of the countries in a sample of borrowers. Using that convention, it can be seen from the debt situation of eighty-four countries surveyed in the 1977 world debt tables that a high debt outstanding in relation to GNP was one in excess of 31 percent in 1975 as against 17.8 percent in 1969, both on a disbursed basis. And a high debt relative to exports of goods and nonfactor services was one in excess of 103 percent in 1969 and 120 percent in 1975.

Next to the relative magnitude of debt outstanding, the size of debt service payments relative to exports can be used as a gauge of the importance of debt. Indeed, it is the most usual yardstick in this respect, one of limited significance, however, and which in any case cannot be relied on in isolation from other indicators.[1]

Just as the debt-export and debt-GNP ratios, the debt-service ratio has been drifing upward: its "high" value for the eighty-four countries increased from 9.7 percent in 1969 to 11.5 percent in 1975. The traditional norm, asserting that difficulties would be likely when the debt-service ratio is in excess of 20 percent, was exceeded by only eight countries in 1975 (Uruguay, Chile, Mexico, Egypt, Peru, Argentina, Sudan, Sri Lanka), most of which indeed either ran into difficulties in 1976 or 1977 or were a serious concern. For that reason, the projected continued increase in this ratio to an average of about 20 percent in 1985 (chapter 8) is somewhat disturbing.

A common feature of these three ratios, and this also holds true of many others, is their skewed distribution. In respect of each ratio, there is a small lead group comprising countries with a high value for that ratio, while the rest lags behind. In 1975, for example, the average of individual debt-exports ratios for eighty-four countries was 92.6 percent while the median ratio was only 69.5 percent. Only a third of the countries recorded ratios in excess of the average.

The lead group, however, does not involve always the same countries. Because the share of exports in GNP varies widely, there is only limited coincidence between a country's ranking for the debt-exports ratio and its ranking for the debt-GNP ratio. Similarly, debt service is not closely related to debt outstanding, because of wide differences in average terms, and rankings in respect of the debt-service ratio can differ strongly from those in respect of the debt-exports ratio. In addition, the composition of the lead group for any given ratio can change rapidly. Zaire, for example, moved from twenty-fourth in 1969 to second in 1975 for the debt-GNP ratio, Zambia from forty-third to ninth. Mexico was number twenty-two in respect of the debt-exports ratio in 1969, up to number nine in 1975, and Zaire again meanwhile moved from fifty-fourth to eleventh. Changes in the opposite direction usually are not as swift; it is easy to get into debt, but getting out of it is something else. Tunisia is one case of a diminishing relative debt: its debt-GNP rank fell from seventh in 1969 to twenty-eighth in 1975 and its debt-exports rank fell from eighth to thirty-seventh. The implication of this variability is that debt situations are apt to change rapidly and that trends in the ratios as well as their absolute values must be monitored.

Another class of ratios relates to the roll-over process. Ratios in this class tend to measure the quality of debt management.

One of them is the refinancing ratio, which measures the share of disbursements that is absorbed by the debt service. For a sample of sixty-nine countries in 1969[2] the average value of that ratio was 69 percent, but the dispersion of individual cases was quite large. In half the cases, the ratio was below 50 percent, while in fourteen countries it was in excess of 100 percent, indicating that these countries at that time paid out more in debt service than they received in new loans. Altogether, no established norm seems to exist for that ratio, the value of which can vary very widely over time depending on available terms and the growth of disbursements.

Also related to the quality of debt management is the maturity structure of debt-service schedules. These should be evenly spread over time to avoid the accumulation of liabilities over a few years, which could cause some liquidity problems. To capture this, scheduled debt-service payments can be discounted and accumulated. Their total is then conceptually analogous to the stock of outstanding debt, allowing, however, for its terms. Were all payments evenly spread over fifteen years, their discounted sum (at a 10 percent rate) would be 50.7 percent of debt outstanding. A greater concentration over the earlier years will result in a higher value for the ratio, and conversely.

By that standard, some bunching of debt service is usual practice. For a sample of twenty-seven countries for which the data were available, the average value of the ratio was 55.5 percent with a rather small dispersion. Only one-fourth of the countries featured ratios in excess of 58.8 percent, which may be taken as a norm indicating the presence of serious bunching problems.

A final indicator deserves mention because its significance extends beyond the scope of debt surveillance: this is the ratio of net transfer over imports, which may be thought of as the "benefit" component of a relation whose "cost" component would be the debt-service ratio.

For the above sample of sixty-nine countries in 1969 that ratio averaged 5.9 percent and was below 9.5 percent in three cases out of four. These are rather low figures. To put them in perspective, they can be compared to the magnitude of export fluctuations: this, according to the IBRD's 1976 world tables,[3] was higher than 9.5 percent for half the developing countries in 1969-1971. In a large number of countries, therefore, export fluctuations represent larger amounts than can be secured through the debt process.

Individual indicators capture only specific facets of the debt process. They do not evidence the process itself. A more comprehensive and also more relevant description can obtain from the simultaneous inspection of several indicators. An obstacle to do this lies in the difference in the ranking of countries for different indicators; a technique is available however, which allows for that difficulty. That technique, called "principal components analysis," relies on graphic tabulation of the complete data set under review. The key to interpreting the charts is that two ratios have a similar role in respect of other indicators when their images on the chart are close together, and conversely. That technique has been applied in the above-mentioned study to a sample of sixy-nine countries, not including those which had to renegotiate their debts, in 1969.

The ten indicators under review are the following: debt service over debt outstanding (DS/DOUT); international reserves over debt (RES/DOUT); debt over GNP (DOUT/GNP); debt over exports (DOUT/X); debt service over exports (DSR); net transfer over imports (NT/M); debt service over disbursements (DS/DISB); disbursements over imports (DISB/M); the growth rate of debt (R) and that of exports (E).

From their location on figure 3-1, these ten ratios can be sorted into three groups, each of which is indicative of a major aspect of the debt process. The first group, located well off to the right on the first (horizontal) axis, provides a composite measure of the degree of exposure to foreign debt. It includes some ratios (DOUT/X, DOUT/GNP, DSR) which are the expression of past reliance on external loans and others (DISB/M and NT/M) which measure current reliance on these loans. Altogether, therefore, the first axis can be considered as an exposure axis.

By the same token, the second axis can be interpreted as a measure of the roll-over conditions. This is because of the presence, well down on the axis and somewhat on the left, of DS/DISB and DS/DOUT, which are indicative of poor roll-over conditions—debt service is high in relation to debt and absorbs a large share of new loans.

The exposure to debt and the roll-over conditions thus appear as the core of a description of the debt status of the sample countries. This clearly suggests a hypothesis about the debt process itself: it is that a balance must be struck between these two major aspects. Large debts can be sustained if the roll-over conditions are favorable; unfavorable roll-over conditions are sustainable if exposure is limited. In other words, the danger area in figure 3-1 would be the zone below the first axis and to the right of the second. Indeed, a plot of the sixty-nine sample countries on that figure, not depicted here, would show that most of them are lying outside that area—and by

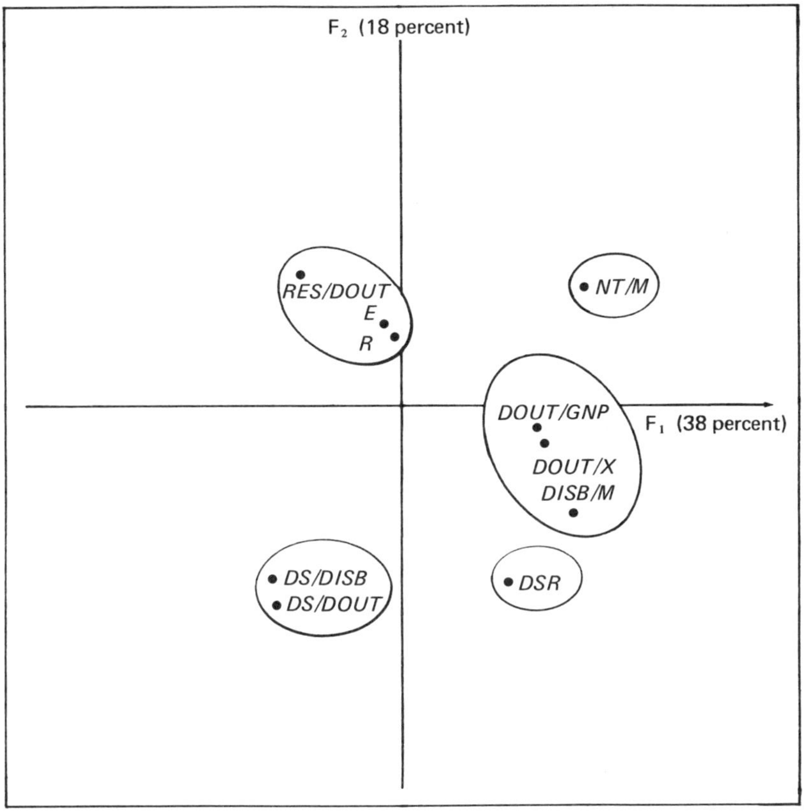

Source: P. Dhonte, "Describing External Debt Situations: A Roll-Over Approach," International Monetary Fund Staff Papers, March 1975, p. 172.

Figure 3-1. Sixty-nine Developing Countries: Relationships Among Ten Indicators

sample construction these countries did not have to renegotiate their debts. A plot of a countersample of twelve renegotiation cases would show most of them within the danger area.

The third group of indicators adds substantially to that interpretation. That group includes the growth rates of debt and exports and the reserves ratio. Disregarding the latter, whose specific role is unclear, the significance of that group lies in the strong correlation between the two growth rates: this can be taken to imply that countries in the sample have struck a balance between the growth of their debt and the growth of their exports. This suggests an additional hypothesis about the debt process: sustainable indebtedness is characterized not only by a balance between exposure and roll-over conditions, but also by a balance between its growth rate and the growth of exports.

Altogether, the experience of sixty-nine nonrenegotiating countries provides an insight into the nature of debt equilibrium. The external debt of a country can be considered well balanced when that country's exposure is matched with adequate terms, resulting in appropriate roll-over conditions, and when its growth is kept in line with the growth of exports. The gist of the matter is that an adequate net transfer should result from appropriate terms, not from a disproportionate growth of disbursements.

This conclusion provides a building stone for the determination of borrowing capacity offered in chapter 6. The approach of that chapter is that a sustainable growth of borrowings is predicated on a matching export performance. Indeed, the previous description of the distribution of external loans suggested that this rationale is instrumental in shaping access to capital markets.

By contrast, the defaulting countries secured an adequate net transfer of resources only through a disproportionate acceleration of disbursements. This can be seen from the experience of thirteen renegotiations involving eleven countries from 1961 to 1970.

Nine of the thirteen cases involved heavily indebted countries. Exceptions (the Philippines, Uruguay, and Yugoslavia in 1971) in part reflected the existence of unrecorded debts. It thus generally seems to take a heavy debt to run into a renegotiation, which is understandable enough. A renegotiation hurts your credit rating and subjects you to relentless foreign intervention; it is not justified for less than significant debts.

The debt levels exceeded by only one-fourth of the countries in the nonrenegotiating benchmark sample in 1969 are the following:

Disbursed debt/exports	86.9 percent
Debt service/exports	9.9 percent
Disbursements/imports	19.0 percent
Net transfer/imports	9.6 percent

Taking these as criteria, although the dates of the renegotiations were diverse, table B-5 shows that the debts of renegotiating countries were usually large. This table also points to several notable features of debt developments in the few years prior to the renegotiation. In most cases, debt outstanding, debt service, and disbursements were increasing rapidly during that period, suggesting some sort of a race with time, all the more notable in view of the frequently high starting points. To take a few recent examples, Chile's debt-service ratio moved from 10.9 percent in 1973 to 28.4 percent in 1975; Uruguay's moved from 22.9 to 45.9 percent for the same dates; and Zaire's moved from 8.5 to 16.5 percent.

Such large and rising ratios reflect debt accumulation disproportionate to export performance, but also engaged on inadequate terms—borrowing short to finance investments with a long payoff period. While some "bunching" of debt-service obligations (that is, some degree of concentration of the schedule over the earlier years) is general practice, that phenomenon was carried to extremes in the renegotiation cases, as debt accumulated on typically short maturities. It has thus been estimated that Ghana's liabilities to Western creditors in 1966 had an average maturity of only six years; close to 75 percent of Zaire's debts at the end of 1975 consisted of debts to private creditors with initial maturities of less than ten years. Likewise, over half of Peru's new borrowings in 1975 and 1976 comprised private commitments with an initial maturity of six years. Contraexamples such as that of Turkey, which ran into problems while its debt was still mostly to official creditors, do not belie the point, as a buildup in short-term liabilities was instrumental in creating an overhang of foreign obligations. Deteriorating maturities indeed seem to be a general feature of crisis situations, resulting in a bunching of problems which necessitated a rearrangement of the debt-service schedule.

Renegotiations: The Diplomatic Experience

Where problems have become intractable, renegotiations have been in order, long, unpleasant, drawn-out experiences of which there are now a large number of instances but still, and this is an important sore point, no established codification. In view of the increased bank lending in developing countries and the attendant increase in the number of defaults involving private banks as creditors, a new dimension has been introduced to the problem, so that official debt settlements must now be distinguished from the rearrangement of debts to private banks.

There have been some thirty-two instances of multilateral rearrangements of official debts from 1959 to 1976, but only eleven borrowers (Argentina, Brazil, Colombia, Chile, Ghana, India, Indonesia, Pakistan, Peru, Turkey, and Zaire) have been involved. This is because in most instances several successive agreements were necessary before a definite solution could be found: this repetition is one feature of the pattern which has evolved from experience.[4]

Requests for debt renegotiations are usually considered at meetings of representatives of the major Western creditors, which are held for the most part in Paris. These meetings are informal; that is, each is convened as an ad hoc session. Nevertheless, because of their frequency and because they all involve essentially the same officials, they have come to be known as "Paris Club" meetings. The Paris Club was first convened in 1956 to facilitate the implementation of a multilateral settlement with Argentina, and has handled all other multilateral official renegotiations since, except those with Turkey (which were held under OECE/OECD auspices), those with Indonesia (which were conducted in The Hague), and those with India, a special case in a number of respects (which took place within a World Bank consortium).

The standard procedure for a debt renegotiation involves first a background evaluation of the size of the defaulting country's debt and its economic prospects. A first meeting is then held among creditors only. The borrower's representatives then participate in a second session, during which the International Monetary Fund is usually called on to give its evaluation of the borrower's stabilization efforts and prospects. A third session convenes creditors to determine the extent of their offer, which is the basis for agreed minutes signed jointly with the borrower. This completes the multilateral stage of the negotiation proper; the guidelines included in the agreed minutes then have to be implemented in bilateral agreements. For that reason a standard feature of the agreed minutes is the provision of a "most favored nation clause," since no lender is, in principle, willing to accept less favorable terms for the stretch-out of its claims than other lenders. Indeed, the provision and enforcement of that clause is one of the major reasons for the existence of a multilateral framework for renegotiation.

Other than this, the substantive contents define the scope of the rearrangement. The debt covered in the renegotiation comprises liabilities to official creditors or officially insured suppliers credits. Because bank loans are not usually officially insured, they cannot be handled within this framework. Not all official debt, however, is necessarily covered in the agreement; successive agreements with Indonesia in 1967, 1968, and 1970, for example, were restricted to debt contracted before July 1966 (table 3-1). Multilateral loans, as a rule, have not been renegotiated either.

The scope of the negotiation is further defined by the identification of the maturities covered in the agreement, that is, the "consolidation period." Usually this has been rather restrictively defined: in many cases, the consolidation period was limited to two years or less, meaning that only those payments originally falling due within those two years could be stretched out. Further, in a number of cases, only a part of the liabilities covered in the consolidation period was consolidated.

Finally, the agreement specifies the repayment terms for the consolidated maturities, including the rate of the moratorium interest.

These provisions can be implemented through rescheduling, refinancing, or debt cancellation. The distinction between the first two is admittedly a fine one. Rescheduling is the more usual practice; it involves the design of a new repayment schedule for those debts covered in the agreement, together with provisions for moratorium interest charges. A grace period is frequently provided for, to allow for the settlement of commercial arrears and/or in expectation of an upturn in the borrower's export performance. Rescheduling does not revise the original loan terms, but provides greater flexibility to meet the foreign exchange transfer. Where the loans have been insured in the creditor countries, the creditor is usually paid under the export credit insurance terms, while the end borrower in the borrowing country is expected to settle its debt in due course with the official agency (usually the Central Bank) responsible for keeping the new timetable.

Refinancing is an alternative technique whereby outstanding obligations are met as initially scheduled, foreign exchange for this purpose being provided from the proceeds of a new loan extended by the creditor countries. Alternatively, repayments may be returned as new loans as original obligations are honored. There is obviously little substantive difference with rescheduling; however, refinancing in some cases may be more easily managed. This has gathered special relevance in the case of private bank loans, as it has avoided the need to classify some loans as losses.

Debt cancellations finally are presently hardly more than a possibility; they have not been practiced in multilateral arrangements, except in some cases for late interest payments. In another context, they are increasingly favored as a goodwill gesture on behalf of the least developed countries.

Beyond these somewhat technical points, the substantive issues involved in multilateral renegotiations relate to the procedures involved and to the respective roles of debt relief and of development assistance. The latter is the more significant point as it commands the former.

As an established position, creditor countries do not consider debt relief as a proper form of development assistance. It follows that the terms of debt relief must be as little concessionary as can be considered consistent with the borrower's economic prospects. Accordingly, most agreements have been fairly restricted in scope; further, in most cases, they have been conditional on the prior implementation of remedial economic policies. In order to make that condition stick, the consolidation period has been defined restrictively, with full knowledge that further renegotiations would be necessary as it expired. Indeed, in many instances there was an explicit or implicit willingness of creditors to reopen negotiations within a short time. This has been dubbed the "short leash" approach to debt relief, surely one of the more irritating features of the process for the borrowers.

The quid pro quo for that position, and an indication of the deep separation of debt relief and development assistance, is the existence of a number of aid coordination groups well separated from Paris Club operations. The distinction was notably exemplified in the case of Indonesia, where after the Sukarno era not one, but two parallel negotiations were initiated, one within the Paris Club to renegotiate outstanding debts and the

Table 3-1
Multilateral Debt Renegotiations, 1956-May 1973

Country and Date of Multilateral Agreement	Scope of Debt Relief: Consolidation Period	Scope of Debt Relief: Type of Debt Covered	Scope of Debt Relief: Proportion of Maturities Consolidated	Scope of Debt Relief: Amount ($ mn.)	Repayment Terms: Grace Period	Repayment Terms: Amortization Period	Repayment Terms: Moratorium Interest Rate	Grant Element of Rescheduling (10% discount rate)
ARGENTINA								
May 30, 1956	Balance, June 30, 1956	Suppliers Credits	100%	500	—	10 years [1]	3½%	23.8%
January 20, 1961	2 years (1/1/61-12/31/62)	(a) Suppliers Credits (principal only) (b) Official loans	50%	284	1 year	5 years	n.a.	n.a.
October 26, 1962	2 years (1/1/63-12/31/64)	Suppliers Credits	50%	174	—	6 years	6%	13.2%
June 26, 1965	1 year (1/1/65-12/31/65)	(a) Suppliers Credits (principal only) (b) Bilateral Official project loans	60%	70	2 years	5 years	6½%	11.5%
BRAZIL								
May 24, 1961	4½ years (6/1/61-12/31/65)	Suppliers Credits	1961—80% 1962—70% 1963—70% 1964—50% 1965—35%	407	6 months	5 years	n.a.	n.a.
July 1, 1964	2 years (1/1/64-12/31/65)	(a) Suppliers Credits covered by 1961 Agreement (b) Suppliers Credits contracted before 12/31/63, with maturity over 6 months	(a) 70% (b) 1964—20% 1965—25%	185	2 years	5 years	n.a.	n.a.
CHILE								
February 24, 1965	2 years (1/1/65-12/31/66)	Suppliers Credits (Principal only)	70%	76	2 years	5 years	5⅞%	15.4%
April 19, 1972	1 year 2 months (11/1/71-12/31/72)	(a) Suppliers Credits (b) Long-term loans of less than 40-years maturity (excl. debt refinancing loans)	70%	278	2 years	6 years	n.a.	n.a.
GHANA								
December 9, 1966	2 years 7 months (6/1/66-12/31/68)	Suppliers Credits	80%	114	2 years 6 months	8 years	6%	23.0%
October 22, 1968	3 years 6 months (1/1/69-6/30/72)	Suppliers Credits covered by 1966 Agreement	80%	84	2 years	7 years 6 months	5¼%	26.3%
July 11, 1970	2 years (7/1/70-6/30/72)	Suppliers Credits covered by 1966 and 1968 Agreements	50%	22	10 years	2 years [2]	—	61.0%

INDONESIA								
December 20, 1966	1 year 6 months (7/1/66-12/31/67)	All public debt [4]	100%					
October 18, 1967	1 year (1/1/68-12/31/68)	Debt covered by 1966 Agreement	100%	1,033	3 years	8 years	n.a.	n.a.
October 17, 1968	1 year (1/1/69-12/31/69)	Debt covered by 1966 Agreement	100%					
April 24, 1970	Balance Outstanding 1/1/70	All public debt, incl. rescheduled contracted before 7/1/66,	100%	2,081	Principal: none Interest: 15 yrs	30 years	—[2]	59.9%
INDIA								
March, 5, 1968 [5,6]	4 years (4/1/68-3/31/72)	All public debt [4]	Variable [3]	407	n.a.	n.a.	n.a.	49.0%
December 27, 1972 [6]	1 year (4/1/72-3/31/73)	All public debt [4]	Variable [3]	151	n.a.	n.a.	n.a.	59.1%
PAKISTAN								
May 26, 1972	2 years 2 months (5/1/71-6/30/73)	n.a.	n.a.	234	2 years	3 years	n.a.	n.a.
PERU								
September 27, 1968	1 year 6 months (7/1/68-12/31/69)	Suppliers Credits	75% (minimum)	146	1-1½ years	4-4½ years	7¼%	9.0%
November 19, 1969	2 years (1/1/70-12/31/71)	Suppliers Credits	60% (minimum)	109	1 year	4 years	8-9%	4.6%
TURKEY								
May 11, 1959	6 years 4 months (8/30/58-1/1/64)	Suppliers Credits	100%	443	none	12 years	3%	27.4%
March 27, 1965	(a) 3 years (1/1/65-12/31/67)	Consolidated Suppliers Credits (principal only)	60%	60	6 years	3 years	n.a.	
	(b) 4 years (1/1/64-12/31/67)	European Fund Credits (principal only)	66-80%	70	Variable	2 years 6 months	3¾%	30.5%
	(c) Variable	Government loans	Variable [3]	90	Variable	Variable	Variable	

Source: Thomas M. Klein, "Economic Aid through Debt Relief," *Finance and Development*, September 1973, p. 20. Reprinted with permission.

[1] Extended to 10 years in 1961.

[2] Interest free, except that 4% interest chargeable on amounts deferred under bisque clause.

[3] Debt relief given mainly through refinancing loans, the terms of which differ.

[4] Debt of the public sector or guaranteed by the public sector in the borrowing country.

[5] The India debt relief arrangements of 1968 originally were for a 3-year period with annual commitments; this procedure was extended for an additional year in June 1971.

[6] Dates are those of a record of understanding reached between consortium members and the Government of India.

other, forming the Intergovernmental Group on Indonesia (IGGI), to provide the required external assistance. Even though a need for assistance was recognized within the IGGI, the short-leash approach was fully adhered to at the Paris meetings, which dragged on for almost four years until a long-term solution was reached in 1970. All payments on public debt falling due until December 31, 1967, were first stretched over eleven years under an agreement of December 20, 1966. On October 18, 1967, similar terms were extended for payments falling due in 1968. Again on October 17, 1968, an extension was granted for payments due in 1969; and it is only in April 1970 that a decision to do away with those yearly renegotiations was reached with an agreement to rearrange all remaining payments on the pre-1966 debt over thirty years.

There are a number of practical reasons for enforcing the short-leash approach to refinancing since in most cases the root of the problem was mismanagement, resulting in a liquidity squeeze, rather than a shortage of external financing holding back the development effort. In a few instances, however, creditors accepted the idea that the latter difficulty was involved, so that debt relief could be considered a form of development assistance. The final Indonesian and Ghanian settlements are relevant in this respect, but the classic case is that of India.

In the case of India, no impending liquidity crisis was looming when creditors agreed in 1968 to a thirty-year rescheduling of part of the debt-service payments due until March 1972. Available flows of external capital on terms acceptable to India were declining, and with rising debt-service payments the net transfer was dwindling. Further, new gross flows were available only in the form of tied aid. By reducing debt-service payments, the net transfer was increased for the same level of gross flows, and the extra foreign exchange made available was not tied.

The Indian approach remains exceptional. The basic principle for official debt relief is that of separation from development assistance. This has also been the basic position of private banks.

In fact, the banks were faced with a wholly new problem when the first serious loan difficulties turned up in 1976. No institutional machinery was available to fulfill the basic Paris Club function of ensuring equal treatment for all creditors; no agreed philosophy was available either on how to handle the cases. In view of the heavy fire of criticism centering on bank lending to developing countries, it also was important for the banks to establish that their involvement was a commercial matter, properly relevant to their normal line of business, and that the whole machinery of risk sharing was working.

In the circumstances, the market was served by the dominating position of a few banks and by the personal leadership of a few bank officers, who insisted on the repayment of debts to private creditors in accordance with contractual agreements in order to maintain creditworthiness for further borrowings.[5] The banks have been very reluctant to call formal defaults,[6] rather allowing some countries to fall in arrears of interest and principal. Accepting a rescheduling was also found to be an unsatisfactory solution, so that the favored arrangement is refinancing, conditional on policy efforts on the part of the borrower.

Renegotiating the Renegotiations

The past experience with debt renegotiations is enough to explain the borrowers' bid to change the rules of the game. Where the renegotiations have been previously conducted by the creditors only, borrowers sought to impose a joint arbitration of borrowers and creditors; where the short-leash approach has been basic, they sought to establish the legitimacy of debt relief as a form of development assistance.

The history of that negotiation, which essentially traces back to the Manila Declaration and Programme of Action of the "Group of 77" in February 1976, is itself a protracted affair, which can be clarified, however, when account is taken of two important points.

The first point is about the developing countries' insistence on the economic environment of debt negotiations, a point designed, of course, to link debt relief and development assistance. The analysis expressed in the Manila declaration is explicit in this respect:

> Heavy debt-service payments, current account deficits stemming from maladjustments in the world economy, inadequate balance-of-payments support and long-term development assistance, coupled with tight conditions and the high cost of loans in international capital markets and difficulties of access to markets in developed countries for exports of developing countries, have all combined to impose a serious and critical strain on the import capacity and reserves of developing countries, thus jeopardizing their development process. The deterioration in the terms of trade of developing countries and the high cost short-term borrowing they have had to resort to recently have seriously aggravated their debt burden. This situation facing the developing countries can be mitigated by decisive and urgent relief measures in respect of both their official and commercial debts.[7]

The gist of that statement is to assert that under the new circumstances arising from the oil crisis the debt problems have global causes and global consequences. They arise not from individual mismanagement but from international maladjustment. They result not only in simple liquidity problems but also in jeopardy of the development process. The implication, as drawn out in the nineteen's proposed resolution to the North-South Conference, is that debt rearrangements should in some circumstances be recognized as an appropriate means of increasing the transfer of untied, quickly disbursable resources to meet the needs of developing countries, and should not be limited to crisis situations.[8]

The argument about the global causes of the current debt situation has drawn some sympathy in developed countries. Some studies suggested, for example, that the recession in industrial countries explains over 55 percent of the deterioration in the current account of developing countries in 1974 and nearly 75 percent of the deterioration over the 1973-1975 period.[9] As noted by World Bank President McNamara, the deterioration in the terms of trade, the recession in industrial countries, and inflation have renewed the dependence of middle-income countries on external capital.[10]

There was little sympathy, however, for the alleged implications of the argument for debt relief. On the contrary, the joint European Community/United States counterproposal to the North-South Conference centered on a formal distinction between the liquidity crisis and the development bottleneck types of debt difficulties—a rather direct reaffirmation that not all debt difficulties make a case for developmental debt relief. Indeed, where balance-of-payments difficulties of a long-term nature impair development, these should, in the view of the developed countries, be considered as resource transfer rather than debt problems.[11]

A second major point in the debate, a familiar one, is the distinction between the poorest (least developed, most seriously affected, landlocked, or island countries) and the other developing countries. That distinction is important because of the marked differences in the composition of debt for these two groups of countries, and also because the scope for adjustment in the poorest countries appears to be more strictly limited than for other countries.

The original Manila Declaration was framed around that distinction. In respect of official debts, it took the view that

> debt relief should be provided by bilateral creditors and donors in the form of waivers or postponement of interest payments and/or amortization, cancellation of principal, etc. of official debt to the developing countries seeking such relief. In that framework the least developed, the developing landlocked and the developing island countries should have their official debts cancelled. Other most seriously affected countries should receive the same treatment or, as a minimum, have their debt service payments on official debts waived until they cease to be regarded by the United Nations as most seriously affected countries.
>
> Multilateral development finance institutions should provide programme assistance to each developing country in an amount no less than its debt service payments to these institutions.[12]

In respect of commercial debt, terms adjustment rather than debt forgiveness was sought:

> Agreement should be reached to consolidate the commercial debts of interested countries and to reschedule payments over a period of at least 25 years. The consolidation of commercial debts and the rescheduling of payments would require the establishment of suitable financial arrangements or machinery, which might include, inter alia, a multilateral financial institution, such as a fund or a bank, designed to fund the short term debts of interested developing countries.[13]

These demands make allowance for the diversity of developing countries. First, they offer separate treatment of commercial and official debt and, within the latter, of the poorest and other countries. Second, the wording of each demand contains a sort of mental restriction, in that the demands would apply only to the developing countries "seeking such relief" or otherwise "interested." These qualifications are in recognition of a divergence within the group among members in the two categories, as fears were expressed by the "commercial" developing countries that pushing the claims too strongly might result in a disruption of their financial relations.

The topic did not really come up for debate at UNCTAD IV in Nairobi, but was discussed at length at the Paris North-South Conference. UNCTAD IV resulted, however, in two resolutions, 94(IV) and 98(IV), dealing with debt problems.[14] Resolution 94(IV) is really little more than a "we are still on speaking terms" resolution, so that the real achievement of UNCTAD IV was to take up the subject again in resolution 98(IV), a resolution dealing with the problems of the poorest countries. This was a step away from a massive all-or-nothing approach that opened up new avenues for negotiation.

As evident from the previous description of key aspects of the proposals put forward at the Paris North-South Conference, little progress was achieved there or at subsequent UNCTAD meetings, and it was not until the March 1978 ministerial session of the Trade and Development Board in Geneva that some agreement could be reached.[15]

Progress during that session was made possible by the adoption of a more selective approach to the problem. The Minister of Trade of Zaire, spokesman for the Group of 77, made a careful differentiation between the official and the commercial debts of the developing countries. He stressed that the proposal for relief related only to official debt, and he suggested that granting of official debt relief to special categories of developing countries in effect only amounted to an extension to past loans of the standards of concessionality currently recognized to be appropriate. Industrial countries, for their part, maintained that debt relief should be provided, if at all, on a case-by-case basis, and they rejected the concept of a generally unmanageable debt of the developing countries. However, they appeared open to the idea of rearranging official development assistance-related debts in the case of the poorest countries as one possible way of providing them with additional assistance. On that basis a compromise was reached, hinging on the fine distinction among relief to the poorest, a response to development needs, and debt relief as such. Relief to the poorest was dubbed "retrospective terms adjustment." It was therefore agreed that developed donor countries will seek to adopt measures for adjustment of terms of past bilateral official development assistance or other equivalent measures as a means of improving the net flows of such assistance. Each donor country will, however, determine the composition and the amounts involved within the context of its own policy.

As an achievement this is a limited one at best, all the more so since it implies that other claims for debt relief, at least in respect of commercial debt, are abandoned. The developing countries, however, have managed to drive some of their points home.

The Geneva agreement, however limited and tentative, does represent a change in approach—the admission of a link between debt relief and development assistance. The practical current scope for that agreement is limited: if fully implemented, it would amount, according to the Swedish (then) Minister of Development, Ola Ullsten, to 0.013 percent of the GNP of members of the Development Assistance Committee. It may not be so unimportant for the countries directly concerned. Further, those countries not directly covered under the agreement are bound to be indirectly concerned too. While debt forgiveness would not be employed in their case, there should be greater flexibility in future debt renegotiations and less of the paternalistic, short-leash approach. Inevitably, greater stock will have to be taken in the development constraints on debt-service capacity when the case of defaulting countries is reviewed.

A second achievement of these negotiations lies in the greatly improved understanding of debt relationships which they have permitted. The scare stories of global default of developing countries have lost much of their weight, and the diversity of individual situations is recognized on both sides. This will help maintain continuity in the flow of capital. It also means, although indirectly, that the developing countries have gained negotiating power. Indeed, the move from an official to a commercial relationship is a move toward a more equal partnership.

In the end, the weight of the facts must be felt. Developing countries can secure a continual net transfer of resources at market terms. This is no assistance; it is a market relationship. And renegotiations in that respect should accordingly remain exceptional. This is a viable proposition, however, only if the economic environment allows for sustained borrowings on those terms. Outright general renegotiations of commercial debts should not be contemplated, but this in turn requires a trade expansion sufficient to maintain adequate borrowing capacity.

4 Creditors Overextended? The Banks

An increasing share of the external debt of developing countries is owed to the international banks, and these liabilities have been built into a significant part of the banks' total assets. That situation is new and has been a cause for concern, especially in 1976 and early 1977.

Indeed, the banks have been very active in recycling oil surpluses and in financing the adjustment of balances of payments in nonoil developing countries. They have exposed themselves in the process and have done so on their own account, as they committed their own borrowed resources. It is therefore reasonable and justified to question the implications for their liquidity structure.

Such concern should, however, be properly circumscribed. The growing bank lending to developing countries may at first have been regarded as a transitory phenomenon, part of the adjustment to the oil price increase; and a number of suspicions have arisen from the view that such activities are abnormal. It is more likely that such lending is not transitory, but amounts to a new fact of life or, to put it emphatically, amounts to a structural change in international relations. Where private international financial intermediation had been restored only among the more industrialized countries, and then only in the late 1960s, it has now been enlarged considerably, so that countries whose only access to external financing was through official channels have gained direct access to private sources.

The Growth of Bank Loans

As indicated in table 4-1, the claims of private financial markets on developing countries amounted to about $180 billion by the end of 1977, or over one-third of the total external claims, net of interbank deposits.

Most of these resources originate from private banks. The achetypal bank loan to a developing country is the medium-term floating-interest-rate syndicated credit. Such a loan is managed by two or three lead banks and subscribed to by a varying number of others, depending on size. It has a specific maturity and amortization schedule, often including a grace period and a "balloon" provision, meaning that the repayments are bunched up in the later periods of its life. Its interest rate is defined by a spread, that is, a margin added on top of a chosen interest rate, which is frequently the London interbank offer rate for the relevant currency as determined by the lead

Table 4-1
Access of Developing Countries to Private Financial Markets, 1976-1977
(billions of U.S. dollars end of period)

	1976	*1977*
External bank claims outstanding		
Latin America	62.3	71.1
Middle East	15.3	22.3
Other Africa	11.7	14.0
Other Asia	34.2	40.9
Southern Europe[a]	15.9	21.8
Total	139.4	170.1
of which: oil producers	(23.1)	(34.6)
Other countries, international institutions and unallocated[b]	190.6	234.9
Grand total[b]	330.0	405.0
Foreign and international bonds[c] issued by		
Developing countries	5.7	10.1
International development institutions	14.6	19.4
Other countries and institutions	78.6	83.7
Total	98.9	113.5

Sources: Bank for International Settlements, *Annual Report,* 1978, chap. 5; and World Bank, *Annual Report,* 1978, appendix table 10.

[a]Greece, Portugal, Spain, Turkey, Yugoslavia.

[b]Net of interbank deposits.

[c]Cumulative gross issues since 1973.

banks. The magnitude of the spread depends on the borrower's credit rating—the spread acts in this respect as a risk/insurance premium. Recent developments have shown, however, that average spreads could be very low—less than 1 percent—suggesting that their average level results from the degree of competition on the market.

Next to the floating-rate credits, some fixed-rate loans are also extended; the relative shares of fixed- and floating-rate financing are not very well known. There has been a recent increase in fixed-rate financing in the form of enlarged subscription by the banks of bond issues of developing countries on their own account. This also indicates that access to the bond markets remains difficult for most of these countries.[1] Indeed, as noted in chapter 1, bond financing is mainly significant as a source of funds to the development institutions.

The access of developing countries to private bank financing itself has been enlarged only recently. This can be ascertained from their share in publicized Eurocurrency credits, an imperfect indicator admittedly, since not all such credits are publicized.[2] Still, an upward trend is clear. International bank loans to developing countries were almost nonexistent in the 1960s. An interest in this field developed among the large banks in the early 1970s. For large projects, syndicated loans became increasingly common, and were largely on behalf of the banks' corporate clients who were investing in developing countries. Syndicated credits in this respect were a substitute for equity investment, notably in the exploitation of mineral resources. Progressively, the banks began to develop lending for their own account and to expand their network of subsidiaries as well; and developing countries accounted for 40 percent of publicized Eurocurrency credits in 1973. This trend was sustained through the oil crisis, and a milestone was laid in 1975 when for the first time (because of a sharp contraction in industrial country borrowing) developing countries borrowed more than industrial countries did, a pattern which was maintained through 1977.

Along with the enlargement of their market share, the developing countries were able to improve their conditions of access to the market, which are now in many cases similar to those available to industrial countries. The difference in terms among the borrowers in these two groups was originally quite sizable: developing countries could obtain longer maturities, but were also charged higher spreads. These differences have been sharply reduced,[4] and the spreads for some countries such as Malaysia and Thailand have become as low as those for industrial countries. Other developing countries such as Bolivia and Panama have been able to break into the fixed-interest bond market, while the few large developing countries with a regular record of borrowing on that market, notably Brazil and Mexico, have made more extensive use of it.

In other cases, private borrowers without a government guarantee have gained access to bank financing, as in the case of a $100 million syndication for the state-owned Pohang Iron and Steel Company of Korea in February 1978.[5] While such loans are not entirely new, they were mostly extended, to date, to oil producers such as Iran. The fact that nonoil developing countries can secure them on a big scale indicates that for some countries at least the trend to a commercial external financial relationship has now run full course.

The role of private banks in developing countries under these conditions is not substantially different from their involvement in the international financing of industrial countries: they are providing financial intermediation rather than a transfer of resources on a net basis. While this trend takes some pressure off the banks, their exposure to developing countries is still a sensitive point in the world financial structure. The reason is that the liabilities of the developing countries to the banks are large, relative to their economic size, and short term, relative to their liabilities to official agencies.

Bank Exposure

The significance of this development is worth stressing. International financial intermediation is not a new phenomenon; it was widespread prior to World War II. France's claims on Russia in the early years of the century, for example, amounted to 12 billion francs, gold francs that is, which would capitalize to about $40 billion today.[6] Argentina's investment income payments exceeded 60 percent of exports in the late 1880s, and those of Australia were above 30 percent throughout the Depression.[7]

Such activity, however, did not involve participating banks in the same fashion as it does today. Banks at the time were acting as intermediaries. They floated notes to the public and collected managerial fees in the process, rather than committing resources at their own risk and collecting interest return. The Russian debt renegotiation may have ruined a number of French households—it did not harm the French banks. Not so today. Since most of the private financing of developing countries is conducted by way of bank loans rather than bond issues, the banks are directly exposed to possible borrower failures in lending to developing countries, as in all international lending.

Assessing their vulnerability is pretty much a matter of guesswork in the absence of detailed information on yield and exposure. However, a number of particular points seem to be rather well established.

First, it would seem that international lending in general and lending to the developing countries in particular have been profitable.[8] This appears to have been notably true of short-term lending, and the increased competition in medium-term lending is sometimes explained as a bid by the smaller banks to get a toehold into that other, more rewarding segment of the market. In Turkey, for example, the foreign banks were rapidly building convertible deposits with Turkish banks in 1977; these are placements of one to two years, with guaranteed foreign exchange at maturity by the Central Bank. These deposits earned substantial front-end fees from the Turkish side or from exporters in the case of trade-related transactions; such fees usually were in excess of 4 percent and sometimes as high as 6 to 7 percent.[9] More generally, with a background of slack domestic demand for credit and difficulties with real estate investment trusts and other tanker ventures, it is widely asserted that most of the profits of U.S. international banks from 1975 to 1976 came from their overseas operations. On the other hand, the growing competition in international credit markets has resulted into a marked reduction in average spreads from 1977 to 1978 which must have sharply reduced profit margins and undermined the stability of the system.[10]

Second, some data also begin to be available about the maturity structure of international bank claims. Recently published breakdowns compiled by the Bank for International Settlements indicate that about half of the claims on developing countries have a residual maturity of less than a year.[11] This is not to say that half the banks' international claims will be paid off on a net basis within a year. Many of the short-term claims are commercial credits which are normally rolled over along with the development of trade flows. Others are financial facilities, for example, balances with correspondent banks abroad, whose level can be expected to be sustained under normal conditions. The short-term nature of these claims is thus more apparent than real.

There is, however, a catch in this respect: such short-term facilities are not well monitored, and experience shows that they tend to build up to unduly large levels when the borrowing country faces a liquidity problem. If that problem develops into a crisis, then an overhang of unaccounted liquid liabilities is discovered, whose resorption much complicates the solution of the crisis. This happened, for example, in Indonesia in 1975 when over $2 billion in new medium-term loans had to be arranged mostly to consolidate the floating of short-term liabilities. More recently, the Turkish convertible deposits have become a general source of embarassment.

Third, it appears that risk evaluation by the lending banks is still far from adequate. While the major banks have eventually made some headway in identifying which countries have excessive debts, the smaller banks have yet to implement their own systems, and all banks still have difficulties in tracking the cases where maturity schedules are unbalanced. Indeed a survey of thirty-seven U.S. banks conducted by the Eximbank indicated that many are dissatisfied with their country risk evaluation procedures and are actively seeking new ones.[12] Furthermore, country risk ratings are only one of the considerations involved in lending decisions, and are not always the dominant one. Commercial or political considerations sometimes wholly extraneous to any preoccupation with solvency are also given great weight.[13]

Against this, the banks can argue that extensive risk-sharing techniques such as syndication, interbank financing, and cofinancing with official agencies limit their exposure to the default of any given borrower or even of any given group of borrowers. Another argument is that the risk involved in country lending differs markedly from ordinary commercial risks; this is the debatable issue of sovereign risk.

Sovereign Risk

While official intermediation is not required for bank loans to developing countries, such lending is not exempt from official or "sovereign" considerations. The risks involved in lending to developing countries, as indeed in all international lending, are "sovereign" in that they depend on the behavior of sovereign entities.

The established argument in this respect stresses the lower chance of outright capital loss when lending to a country, because unlike a firm, a country is not likely to go under because of excessive debt. The lender would thus be faced with a liquidity problem (rather than a loss) until its claims could be liquidated. This may be an overly fine distinction. Unless a default is to be called, refinancing must be arranged. However, refinancing, as distinguished from normal rollover, exists only when the banks are cornered into accepting substandard terms to protect their original investment; it is a disguised, stretched-out loss, at least in the form of forgone income. It may turn out to be less costly than a writeoff, so the difference is in degree, not substance.

More substantively, sovereign risk differs from ordinary commercial risk in several significant respects. One of these involves sovereignty as a qualification of the liquidity risk, one of the ways in which illiquidity can materialize. This is first because the conditions that may require a rearrangement of the loan payment schedule are macroeconomic in character. It is not enough that the project for which a cross-country loan is nominally extended should yield a proper return; it must also be that the economy as a whole can manage the debt service. Any cross-country loan is ultimately a balance-of-payments support loan. The reverse, however, is not necessarily true: lending to an unsound corporate entity can lead to problems even if the economy is globally balanced.

Further, the decision to default, or rather the decision to take the measures necessary to avoid a default, is a political one.[14] Similarly, where the governments of creditor countries have large economic and political stakes, they may mount a rescue operation rather than let a borrower default on its obligations to private creditors.[15] An odd case of history repeating itself illustrates the point. A factor which caused much friction in Peru's 1967 debt difficulties was the government's decision to purchase some French military aircraft; a factor causing a fair amount of irritation in Peru's 1977 debt difficulties was the government's decision to buy some Russian military aircraft.

Sovereignty also implies more than a qualification of the liquidity risk: it may result in a properly political involvement of the banks.[16] Restoring normal conditions after a failure involves the same broad macroeconomic and political considerations as are instrumental in bringing about that failure. As a consequence, safeguarding their loans draws creditors into the exercise of global power over the defaulting country, and this may be a serious problem for the banks themselves.

Indeed, history is littered with cases of foreign creditor intervention, from the Mexican war of the Second French Empire to the Turkish and

Egyptian takeovers of the turn of the century, to a number of contemporary cases. It was, for example, a foreign consulting firm, Arthur Young and Associates, which was called in to clear up Pertamina's administrative chaos, while Kuhn, Loeb, Lazard Freres, and S.G. Warburg were commissioned as financial advisors to Bank Indonesia. The same group of foreign investment banks also stepped in to sort out the external debt of Gabon and advise on policies to get out of the mess. In Zaire, foreign creditors insisted that very senior positions be held by appointed foreigners. And in Peru, a $220 million loan in August 1976 was tied to a detailed policy understanding designed by the participating banks.

Finally, cross-country lending imposes some properly international responsibilities on the banks. Just as they fulfill a global function in the international adjustment process by lending to developing countries, their reactions to possible difficulties could have extensive repercussions. The stake here is to resist the temptation to reduce their exposure in the face of a default, a temptation which is very strong. Such an attempt would further compromise the borrower's chances of recovery. Pressing for excessively harsh adjustment measures must also be resisted, and not just on ethical grounds. Such an attitude might simply be unrealistic where a single borrower is concerned. Where a number of them are simultaneously involved, it could result in cumulative effects detrimental to the expansion of world trade.

Sovereign risk, however, is not confined to lending to developing countries. It is a characteristic of all international lending. The difference in lending to industrial countries is that the extent of economic and political integration of these countries allows strongly discounting the sovereign aspects of the liquidity risks. In addition, these countries are not nearly as indebted, relative to their size, as developing countries. On the other hand, as the experiences of Great Britain and Italy have indicated, severe strains occurring in these countries could have extensive repercussions.

Market Regulation

The shock caused by the failure of the German bank Herstatt in 1974 had a profound influence in establishing tighter, less competitive market conditions, with fewer banks operating and larger spreads and shorter maturities for all borrowers. Lending to the developing countries, however, was not at stake.

Actual concern about lending to developing countries as such became widespread in 1976 and early 1977. The average spread differential rose to 0.29 percent in 1976, and maturities turned slightly unfavorable. Concern was heralded on the occasion of testimony given to the Senate Banking

Committee by the comptroller of the currency, reporting large amounts of international loans extended by major U.S. banks and classified as substandard, doubtful, or losses.[17] It came to be rather widely held that defaults were inevitable. Indeed, Argentina, Zaire, and Indonesia were already falling into arrears, Peru was coming in line as a trouble spot, others were looking uncertain.

A crucial test was provided by Zaire, a country which with its low per capita income and general level of development would not normally have qualified for bank financing. The banks were caught out of bounds when Zaire, after more than a year of default on both principal and interest, rescheduled its debts to governments and banks guaranteed by governments in June 1976. They were faced with the issue of agreeing to a similar settlement or insisting on compliance with original contractual arrangements. The case was all the more decisive because over a hundred banks from many countries were involved who wanted to avoid a writeoff (this could have cast doubt on all their international operations) and a rescheduling (which might have set a precedent for other borrowers).[18]

In the event the test was passed—not too well, though, in the case of Zaire. Crises have been handled as they arose, defaults have been consolidated, new loans have been forthcoming. By the end of 1977, bank lending to developing countries gained acceptance as an established fact. Still, with many trouble spots still looming, there was much soul searching within the industry and its regulatory agencies about the definition of some kind of official support and safeguards for these operations. Various ideas have been considered in that connection.

One approach calls for official surveillance of bank exposure. This approach is being enforced in the United States by the Federal Reserve and the comptroller of the currency, along different inclinations, however. While the comptroller is inclined to establish his own country ratings as a basis on which to evaluate the quality of bank assets, the Federal Reserve would rather rate the banks' lending policy, including notably the quality of their risk evaluation procedures, and the degree of geographic risk concentration.[19]

Another, more controversial approach involves the international agencies, especially the International Monetary Fund and the World Bank. These agencies have the information and the expertise required for a proper assessment of country risk; they also have the capacity to design remedial policies and to oversee their implementation when trouble brews.

One possible way to make use of these resources is to provide the banks with inside information, that is, with the agencies' assessment of borrowers' policies. That suggestion has been brushed aside by the agencies, who feel that they have a bond of confidence to their member governments and who fear that publicizing their evaluations might impair their staff's work.[20] Exceptions to this rule are made, however, with the borrower's consent in the case of cofinancing arrangements or when the IMF is called in to provide a description of borrower's policies in debt renegotiations.

A more effective avenue of cooperation has been the development of cofinancing between the World Bank and private banks. Cofinancing has been a long-standing practice between official agencies or in combination with suppliers' credits. Its extension to private financial sources is rather recent and remains limited to a number of large projects, although it may become more frequent in the future.[21]

A third suggestion is to give the IMF a regulatory role, to prevent excessive lending by the private banks or to impose remedial policies on their behalf. Again, this idea has elicited a very skeptical response from the institution. Of course, the IMF long has been in the business of designing remedial policies under its stand-by arrangements, and indeed a fair part of its muscle is linked to the role of these arrangements in facilitating the access to private bank financing. It is, however, by no means the case that the banks have always taken shelter behind such arrangements, even in difficult cases, and the IMF shuns an explicit assignment of that sort.

The reluctance of the agencies is understandable. The commercial activities of private banks should not be confused with the development assistance assignments of the World Bank or with the IMF's responsibility to maintain orderly market conditions. The banks and their regulatory agencies should avoid overlending as well as panic reactions in the face of crises; they cannot control the economic environment, however. Because they are extended on market terms, bank loans must be supported by rapidly growing exports: this is where the international institutions can be of assistance.

Part III
The Limits to Debt

A topical question in view of recent experience is whether high growth rates of debt can be sustained. That question may call for a simple answer, as long it is clearly understood that debt is an ongoing process, not just a balance sheet figure.

A country can borrow abroad for a number of immediate reasons: a dam to build, a crop that failed, and so on. Underlying them all is a common concept: spend more than you earn, import in excess of your exports, invest over your savings. All this calls for a foreign resource transfer. Debt is one way to secure it, but it is not an unspecific way.

Debt is no end in itself. It is a means to an end, which is to secure additional foreign purchasing power. Thus it only makes sense if new borrowing always remains in excess of interest and amortization payments.

Initial borrowings, or the initial acceleration of disbursements, yield some leeway. Shortly repayments come to maturity, they are covered through further borrowing, and so on. The point is that a steady increase in disbursements must be managed, at a quick enough pace to keep abreast of service payments and still in a manner restrained enough to keep the system under control.

The difficulty is to stay clear of two hazards. The first is that of the avalanche, that of letting debt increase out of proportion with the borrower's economic base. Disbursements cannot increase rapidly to a country whose exports languish; the growth of debt must keep in step with export growth.

The second hazard is suffocation. When disbursements only creep forward, new loans hardly cover the debt-service payments. What remains to the borrower becomes minimal—it may well become negative, in fact, allowing for interest payments. Then why bother if the whole complicated operation does not even yield a significant net transfer?

There is a ceiling to the growth rate of debt, and there is a floor: there lies the problem of debt. The simultaneous operation of these two constraints imposes a limit on borrowing capacity: you can borrow only so much now if you can borrow more later.

That equilibrium must hold for any debt level, but it can hold for various levels. Debt management is thus faced with two basic questions: that of the limits to debt over time and that of its limits at any time.

5 Why Borrow?

Countries can differ in their reliance on external debt; in all cases, their policies must be consistent, since it is always just as difficult to bail out of debt as it is easy to get into it. For that reason, to borrow abroad is a major political decision.

A fairly large theoretical investment has been addressed to that decision, resulting notably in the development of "growth cum debt" models. The practical conclusion of that effort is that foreign borrowing, on whatever scale it is undertaken, should first and foremost be conducted in a sustainable manner. A significant body of opinion, however, holds that the best policy is an outright rejection of the use of debt.

No Debt as the Best Debt

A first guideline is offered by those who hold that the best debt is no debt at all. They do not fuss about technical detail but take debt for what it is, a strategic choice that durably commits the society and economy of the borrower. They question the very foreign exposure which reliance on foreign debt inevitably entails. In their view, international trade has all too often been unequal in nature, resulting in distortions in the domestic economic structure of developing countries, as the eruption of cheap, elaborate foreign goods destroyed the social fabric of these countries.[1] This is the point of departure of a forceful criticism of the International Monetary Fund by Payer. In her analysis, "aid" is the counterpart of the liberalization of imports, which she sees as the heart of the IMF's stabilization programs. The gamble of many governments is that aid will more than pay for the cost of the additional, nonessential imports: "Many hard pressed governments have believed the gamble was worth taking . . . they were guilty of misjudgment."[2]

The strength of these arguments lies in their global character: external borrowing is indeed a political decision, and the designation of "sovereign loans" is very proper. For all its merits, the international division of labor can be misused. In a number of cases, reliance on external trade and external financing has been associated with initiatives on the part of foreign interests or of minority groups in the borrowing country rather than with a concern for a broadly based domestic development using locally available techniques and stressing self-reliance.

The case against debt must therefore be given consideration at the proper political level. This does not detract from the opportunity to establish the technician's case for debt; rather, it adds to it. The implication, however, is that the "economic" answer, as regards the determination of optimal debt, is just that: a technician's answer.

The Case for Debt

The economic case for debt rests on its contribution to accelerated growth. External resources can accelerate growth by adding to the country's investment capacity. They can also provide compensation for export fluctuations and assist in the intermediation of domestic savings. Compensatory financing, however, is in principle reversed as exports rebound, and financial intermediation as such does not involve a net transfer of resources other than for the payment of service fees. The basic case for debt is therefore related to a long-run development perspective in which a sustained inflow of external resources adds to domestic investment. That case has been established notably by Chenery and Strout and bears the mark of their original formulation, which was laid in terms of net resource transfer rather than of debt flows. It calls accordingly for additional consideration of the specific properties of debt as an instrument for a net transfer of resources.

The heart of the Chenery and Strout study is to determine how foreign resources can contribute to development. In their view, development requires a simultaneous increase in several factors—labor, skills, savings, export earnings—not all of which are equally available at one given time. The relatively scarce factors create bottlenecks, resulting in underutilization of other inputs. The role of foreign assistance is to relieve these constraints and to allow for higher growth by permitting a fuller use of available resources.[3]

It is assumed that given some technological constraints, a minimum investment ratio is required to achieve a given growth target. In the absence of foreign resources, investment and growth are constrained by available savings at the current income level. As production increases, savings also rise; and with a well-behaved savings function the savings ratio can improve. Investment therefore picks up and production accelerates. That process, however, is time-consuming.

This process can be sped up when foreign resources make it possible from the start to raise investment to the level required for a chosen growth target. This does not require an indefinite inflow of foreign capital: as long as the marginal savings rate is in excess of the required investment ratio, a time will come when the flow of resources can be reversed, still allowing for sustained growth. Aid requirements are therefore limited both over time and at any moment, depending on the chosen growth target and the values of the relevant savings and investment parameters, but depending also on the appropriateness of the domestic development policies. Foreign assistance is a booster of, not a substitute for, self-help. In the long run, the use that is made of the initial increase in output is essential; the economy will not become self-supporting unless the additional output is allocated so as to increase saving and reduce the trade gap.

Given proper economic management, a time will come when the borrower will be able to sustain high growth at the target level without further external assistance and eventually to reverse the flow of foreign aid, although the expected duration of the cycle is a long one, spanning several decades.

There could be a risk though that foreign aid might substitute for domestic savings rather than add to them; to that extent, its efficiency as a booster of economic growth would be curtailed. Such substitution could affect savings or the external trade of the recipient country.

The substitution of foreign for domestic savings is likely to happen, but only to a limited extent. Weisskopf has shown that foreign capital has an adverse direct influence on the national savings ratio.[4] Looking for empirical evidence, however, he finds that the substitution would apply only in the countries where savings rather than foreign exchange is the constraint on growth. In a number of these cases, no substitution seems to happen; where it happens, it cancels about one-quarter of the inflow of foreign resources. In addition, even where the domestic savings ratio is reduced by the substitution effect, ex post savings may well increase because of the larger level of output resulting from the use of the foreign resources. Altogether, there is a risk that "leaks" will develop, which undermine the efficient use of foreign resources; but it is unlikely that they are large enough to make these resources inefficient. Again, much depends not only on the volume of foreign resources, but also on the use which is made of the extra output.

The possible adverse effect of aid on foreign trade is a slightly more involved question. In short, it amounts to this: in the absence of foreign capital, a country balances its accounts for a given exchange rate. In the presence of foreign capital, the balance will hold for a higher rate, allowing for a trade deficit. A higher exchange rate, however, will be adverse to the production of export goods or import substitutes; the loss of foreign exchange in that fashion would cancel out part of the inflow of foreign capital.

For members of the structuralist school, that eventuality can be discounted. In their view, the rigidity of the developing economies is such that a possible overvaluation of the currency resulting from capital inflows is immaterial. The production of exports would be constrained by demand on foreign markets, while the domestic economy would lack the flexibility to reallocate resources between the production of domestic goods and import substitutes. Thus a devaluation would not result in greater output of international goods, and the overvaluation case is an abstraction.

The structuralist position is a rather extreme one, for it implies that some countries, no matter how they try, would be unable to balance their external accounts. While it is true that primary producers may be faced with inordinately adverse situations because of unfavorable market developments for their export commodities, the experience of a number of countries shows that large shifts can be achieved in the composition of domestic output and exports. Further, even in the case of extreme rigidity of resource allocation, external balance can be obtained by reducing the absorption of imports, a result that can be achieved through the adverse terms of trade effects of a devaluation.

The overvaluation problem is thus a real one. However, while it can be corrected through a devaluation, the cure cannot leave the level and the growth of income unchanged, because of its adverse terms of trade implications.[5]

Even though it may result in an overvaluation bias, foreign assistance is therefore not inefficient, since the alternative lower exchange rate without foreign assistance would also require a lower growth rate. In addition, over time, the added economic activity generated by the use of foreign resources increases import absorption, thus reducing the overvaluation bias. Still, an obvious and very real difficulty is to draw the line between the particular form of overvaluation which accommodates a planned capital inflow and the perverse case where the capital inflow instead accommodates a fundamental disequilibrium.

In the Articles of Agreement of the World Bank, an attempt was made to distinguish among these cases by identifying development lending with productive projects only. Accordingly, an exchange rate could be considered inappropriate if the capital inflow attracted by rates of return higher than the international cost of capital is not sufficient to bring the supply of foreign exchange in line with imports.[6] Aid proper, that is, the provision of loans at preferential interest rates, does therefore generate a distortion of some sort. Unless it is to be self-defeating, its use must be accompanied by specific adjustment measures in order to compensate the effects of the overvaluation on the domestic economic structure. In fact, in most debt crises, an overvaluation is found to exist, suggesting that the problem is a delicate one to handle.

How Much Debt?

Granting with the above caveats that foreign capital can accelerate economic growth, the question becomes how to find out the extent to which it should be relied on. This question can be answered in several ways, depending on which aspects of the problem are emphasized.

A straightforward solution is contained in the Chenery and Strout approach: set a growth target, compute the investment level required for that target and the available savings at the going income level, and secure what is missing. This, however, really determines the net transfer requirements for a given growth target; no allowance is made for the use of debt as such as a specific way to obtain that net transfer.

Allowance for debt as such is made in the "interest rate versus rate of return" approach, which may be the basic theoretical answer to the question posed. Since foreign resources do not come free, they can be profitably borrowed only if their rate of return—net of all possible perverse effects on savings and the domestic economic structure—exceeds the interest rate. Beyond that point, additional resources could still increase domestic output, but not enough to match interest payments, so that national income would, in fact, be reduced.

There have been extensive discussions of this approach in the literature, with notable contributions from Hayes, Quayum, and Ball,[7] among others. The discussion has largely centered on the determination of the macroeconomic measure of the rate of return, allowing for the direct impact of the foreign resources on growth through investment and their indirect impact through the effects of growth on savings. The object of the exercise is to specify the "critical interest rate" which a country can profitably accept for its foreign borrowings. Under this approach, borrowing capacity depends on the availability of external funds at or below the critical interest rate. That amount may well fall short of that which is required to achieve a given growth target. This provides a rationale for official assistance on concessional terms.

Debt financing, however, also requires that considerable attention be given to the time dimension of the process. As indicated in the review of the "casualties," great leaps forward do not pay. On the contrary, numerical simulations of the duration of the debt cycle, as in Hayes, and empirical estimates, as in Finch,[8] suggest that the growth-cum-debt process spans very long periods. For example, the U.S. investment service ratio exceeded 10 percent for over sixty years from 1850 to World War I. For all relevant purposes, the practical approximation of the debt cycle within any given planning period is linear; no planning period is long enough to allow for the redemption of external debt. Since the maturities of external loans are shorter than the span of the development cycle, debt service on old loans must be paid out of the proceeds of new ones. However, while the takeoff is in progress, a continued net transfer must be secured. Altogether, current loans conflict with the net transfer of future periods and should not be allowed to grow to the point where they would put the net transfer in jeopardy. A relevant imposition on borrowing policies is that they should be sustainable over time.

This is the basis for a third approach to optimal debt, as developed by Loser: borrow as much as you can, provided that you can keep borrowing at that rate:

> The management of external debt should aim at providing the maximum net transfer that can be sustained over time, while other policies must provide for a current account outcome consistent with access to foreign borrowing over the medium term.[9]

This is also the starting point for the pragmatic position taken here.

6 Borrowing Capacity: Soft Terms or Rapid Growth

There is a very wide range of debt ratios among developing countries. India's debt in 1975 was over four times its exports, but the ratio was only 6 percent for Singapore. Uruguay's debt-service payments that year were equivalent to almost half of its exports, while those of Gambia were less than 1 percent.

More significantly, the limits to debt are very puzzling. Indeed, when they arise, problems mostly concern heavily indebted countries; but many others manage at equally high debt levels and do not run into a renegotiation.

All this indicates how practical is the question of evaluating a country's borrowing capacity. This question is considered here in the framework of financing economic development. Were it only a matter of compensatory financing of exports fluctuations or crop failures, the situation would be different: drawings of one year could be paid off the following year. This is not so when the purpose is to accelerate development. That takes a continued transfer of resources, not just a push; whatever the policy, it has to be lasting. This is a major lesson from the policy experience of defaulting countries.

As indicated in chapter 3, these countries accumulated their debts at a rate and under terms which could not be sustained. Their rising debt-service obligations required an increase in disbursements beyond credible proportions or else the acceptance of a negative net transfer. Neither solution was palatable: they went into debt difficulties because they did not give sufficient consideration to the need to sustain their borrowing policies over time. Their difficulties can be traced to the loans contracted before the difficulties became apparent. At that time, however, they were able to borrow excessively, with lenders happily concurring. Borrowing capacity is not constrained by immediate limits to the access to financial sources; the relevant constraint operates over time.

A further lesson from the experience of defaulting countries is that the deterioration was sudden and fairly unexpected by lenders and borrowers alike. Any viable debt policy must be forward-looking; it must be based not on current ratios or those of the recent past, but on those which will prevail in a few years. This is probably one of the major shortcomings of most debt indicators: what they describe already belongs to the past. A suitable "forward" debt-service ratio will be one which describes the debt status that will emerge in the future out of present policies, rather than the current debt status resulting from past policies.

Borrowing Capacity Defined

There are limits to debt, but the right way to find out about them is not to look for ceilings on outstanding debt or debt service, for that could even prove misleading. The right way is to look for ceilings on annual borrowing commitments. Current borrowings determine future debt service and should be restrained by whatever restraint is imposed on it. The limit to debt is not properly expressed by a figure for a given ratio. By nature, it is a requirement of consistency between current policies and long-term ceilings on debt. What really matters is not the specific ceiling which is aimed for, but whether current policies are, in fact, consistent with any given limit. And as long as they are, there may be a fair amount of flexibility in setting the ceiling.

The real problem, therefore, is to determine borrowing capacity rather than debt-bearing capacity. Borrowing capacity is essentially restricted by two factors. First, again, it must be consistent with a ceiling for debt. Whether that ceiling is defined in terms of debt service or debt outstanding is not an essential point; the more usual practice is to refer to the debt-service ratio. The substantial point is that pegging actual borrowings at capacity level and keeping them there should result in the long run in a stable level of debt, not an ever-rising one. This, of course, is meaningless in dollar terms: stable levels mean stable *relative* to the borrower's economic base.

That debt cannot indefinitely grow faster than the borrower's economy is understandable enough. In view of the problems of financial and economic management involved in the conduct of borrowing policy, not to mention the political constraints, some upper tolerance level must exist. That level will presumably be lower when the financing comes in the form of tied or project loans, because of the increased managerial problems for these loans. It will also vary from country to country, since some, such as Brazil, Zaire, the Ivory Coast, and Panama, have a rather favorable attitude toward foreign borrowing which others, such as India, Kenya, and Nigeria, do not share.[1] Besides, even as borrowers might be willing to increase their reliance on debt, lenders may not have the same inclination. As indicated in chapter 2, some exposure limits are defined, however flexibly, for each borrower, so that a country with inordinately large reliance on debt would be likely to hit a supply constraint.

The second constraint is that borrowings should not be allowed to be cut down. Borrowing a lot today, with the faint resolve of borrowing less tomorrow, is a permanent temptation which should not be indulged. Development is a time-consuming process, and continuity is essential. Ample evidence to the contrary is offered by the borrowing policies of defaulting countries. Indeed, access to foreign capital must increase over time until the need for a net transfer vanishes.

Borrowing capacity is defined by the joint operation of two constraints: borrowings are within capacity if they can be maintained permanently at their current level without resulting in an excessive debt-service ratio. *Borrowing capacity* is the highest level of borrowings, relative to exports, that can be maintained indefinitely while the debt-service ratio is kept below a stated limit.

As with the ceiling on debt, borrowing capacity is expressed as a percentage of the borrower's economic base. Exports are selected as the relevant measure in this respect. Other candidates such as GNP might be used, notably in the framework of growth-cum-debt models. Indeed, in some empirical applications that variable was found to perform better than exports. Nevertheless, exports are considered here, on the grounds that external debt is an international economic relationship and that exports are more relevant than GNP for its management, notably to evaluate the liquidity problems arising from export fluctuations.

Expressing the ceiling and the borrowing capacity as percentages of exports also implies that both will grow over time at the same rate as exports. Indeed, that growth rate plays a major role in the determination of borrowing capacity. This does not preclude short-term variations in the reliance on debt over time. Even as a matter of trend, there may be increased reliance because of the progress in financial intermediation; as experience with foreign debt is gained, tolerance levels will rise. Relaxing the conclusions is easy enough analytically and does not change their thrust, so this trend will not be accounted for here. The essential point is that in all cases borrowing capacity is not a unique figure but depends on the environment, that is, in the present formulation, on the growth rate of exports.

The Determination of Borrowing Capacity

Under the above definition, bororowing capacity first increases along with the ceiling on debt. This is a trivial point: the higher the level of debt that is judged to be acceptable, the higher the level of borrowings consistent with it, other things being equal. A number of qualifications are in order in this respect.

Two other variables are essential to determine borrowing capacity for a given ceiling on debt: these are the terms of the loans and the growth rate of exports (in that it imposes a constraint on the growth rate of disbursements).

For a given debt-service ratio, borrowing capacity is larger when terms are softer and when the growth rate of exports is higher. This is the result of the mechanics of debt.

Given a ceiling on debt service, borrowing capacity directly depends on the share of new loans which is absorbed by debt-service payments, that is, on the refinancing ratio. Thus if that share is one-half and a decision is made not to allow the debt-service ratio to exceed 10 percent, then the borrowing ratio can be set at 20 percent. The question then is to determine the refinancing ratio.

A difficulty with this is that present borrowings are not as much related to current as to future debt service. That question is much simplified, however, because of the requirement that borrowing policies be sustainable. A given ceiling on the debt-service ratio will be durably respected only when debt service grows at the same rate as exports; and this (allowing for an adjustment period equal to the average maturity of the loans) holds only if borrowings under given unchanging terms also grow at that rate. Once these conditions hold, all debt figures grow apace, and the relation of present disbursements to future debt service gives way to a structural relation between the disbursements ratio and the debt-service ratio. Netting out exports on both sides, that relation is nothing but the refinancing ratio which is therefore a structural characteristic of a borrowing policy engaged on stated terms and sustained at a given growth rate, not a projection of future developments. The policy may change in the future, but that does not detract from the relevance of considering its structural characteristics.

As indicated in appendix A, the refinancing ratio can be expressed easily enough as a function of the growth rate and the terms of the loans. As an illustration, table 6-1 gives its values under alternative assumptions for these variables.

As can be seen from that table, the refinancing ratio exceeds 100 percent in all cases where the growth of disbursements is lower than the interest rate. This is an application of Domar's law[2] that disbursements will remain in excess of debt service only if their growth rate is in excess of the interest rate.

Under other assumptions, debt service is found to "eat up" widely different shares of disbursements. For a given growth rate, that share is lower for softer terms; for a given terms assumption, it is lower for higher growth rates of disbursements.

While the influence of terms is well known, the original feature of table 6-1 is to show the simultaneous influence of the growth rate of disbursements. The relation is somewhat complex but lends itself to some simplification. First, the influence of all three variables operates in the same direction: lower interest rates, longer maturities, and a stronger growth of disbursements all make for a lower refinancing ratio. Their cumulative in-

Table 6-1
Refinancing Ratio[a] under Alternative Assumptions
(percent)

	Growth Rate of Disbursements				
	5	*10*	*15*	*20*	*30*
Maturities of 5 years					
Interest: 2	93.0	83.0	74.3	66.9	55.0
6	102.4	91.3	82.3	74.4	61.4
10	115.2	100.0	90.1	81.6	67.8
Maturities of 10 years					
Interest rate: 2	87.2	70.6	58.2	48.9	36.2
6	104.2	85.5	71.2	60.2	45.4
10	121.3	100.0	83.9	71.6	54.4
Maturities of 20 years					
Interest rate: 2	77.9	54.6	40.8	32.1	22.2
6	107.5	77.2	59.0	47.2	33.3
10	136.8	100.0	77.2	62.3	44.4

Source: Appendix A.
[a]Ratio of debt service over disbursements.

fluence therefore is sizable. Second, the range of variation of these variables is not, in fact, quite as large as shown in table 6-1, notably because lenders adjust somewhat the terms to economic performance. Accordingly, within the more usual range, as suggested from the data in table 6-3, the influence of maturities is relatively small, and a fair approximation of the complete formula obtains from the following relation:

$$\frac{\text{Debt service}}{\text{Disbursements}} = 1 - 0.1 \frac{\text{growth rate of disbursements}}{\text{interest rate}}$$

This approximate formula sheds light on the important role of the growth rate of disbursements in relation to the interest rate, and also shows that the refinancing ratio can be interpreted as an extension of Domar's law. The roll-over process will be conducted all the more easily when the growth rate of disbursements is well in excess of the interest rate. More generally, there is a tradeoff between export growth and the terms; countries with a lower export growth can achieve the same refinancing ratio as other countries if they are given access to softer terms. This provides a rationale for the terms adjustments of official lenders and shows that only the high-performing countdies have sustainable access to private financial markets.

The significance of the refinancing ratio for borrowing capacity is immediate: for any ceiling on the debt service ratio, borrowing capacity is equal to that ceiling times the inverse of the refinancing ratio. The result is illustrated in table 6-2 for the case where the interest rate is 6 percent and the ceiling on the debt-service ratio is set at 20 percent. The growth rate of disbursements is taken to be the same as that of exports, and the table indicates the level of disbursements consistent with the ceiling and other conditions, that is, borrowing capacity. As can be seen from figure 6-1, borrowing capacity is strikingly larger for the countries with a strong export performance. A country with a 20 percent annual export growth, for example, can borrow half more in ten-year loans as a country with a 10 percent export growth—and still the two would have the same debt-service ratio. The difference in net transfer therefore is huge: the first country will have a net transfer four times as large, relative to its exports, as the second.

The second part of table 6-2 gives the debt ratio resulting from full use of borrowing capacity under the same assumptions. As shown in figure 6-2, export growth here exercises only limited influence: while they can sustain much larger borrowings, countries with a strong export growth do not find themselves saddled with much heavier debts, because their performance rapidly discounts past net flows relative to current exports. The influence of maturities, however, is very strong in all cases, explaining the presence, among the lead group of countries with a high debt-exports ratio, of a large number of recipients of official assistance.

Altogether, because the growth of disbursements heavily influences the refinancing ratio and because disbursements cannot lastingly increase much more rapidly than exports, countries have widely differing borrowing capacities, depending on export performance.

Table 6-2
Borrowing Capacity under Alternative Assumptions[a]
(percent)

Growth Rate of Exports	*Borrowing Capacity[b]* Maturities: *5 years*	*10 years*	*20 years*	*Debt Outstanding[c]* Maturities: *5 years*	*10 years*	*20 years*
5 percent	19.6	19.2	18.6	45.0	82.0	140.0
10 percent	21.9	23.4	25.9	46.6	86.3	147.0
15 percent	24.3	28.1	33.9	48.1	90.4	154.4
20 percent	26.9	33.2	42.4	49.6	94.1	159.9
30 percent	32.6	44.1	60.1	52.3	100.5	166.7

Sources: Table 6-1 and appendix A.
[a]Assumes a 20 percent ceiling on the debt service ratio and an interest rate of 6 percent.
[b]Maximum disbursements ratio consistent with note a and other table assumptions.
[c]Debt outstanding as percentage of exports assuming full use of borrowing capacity.

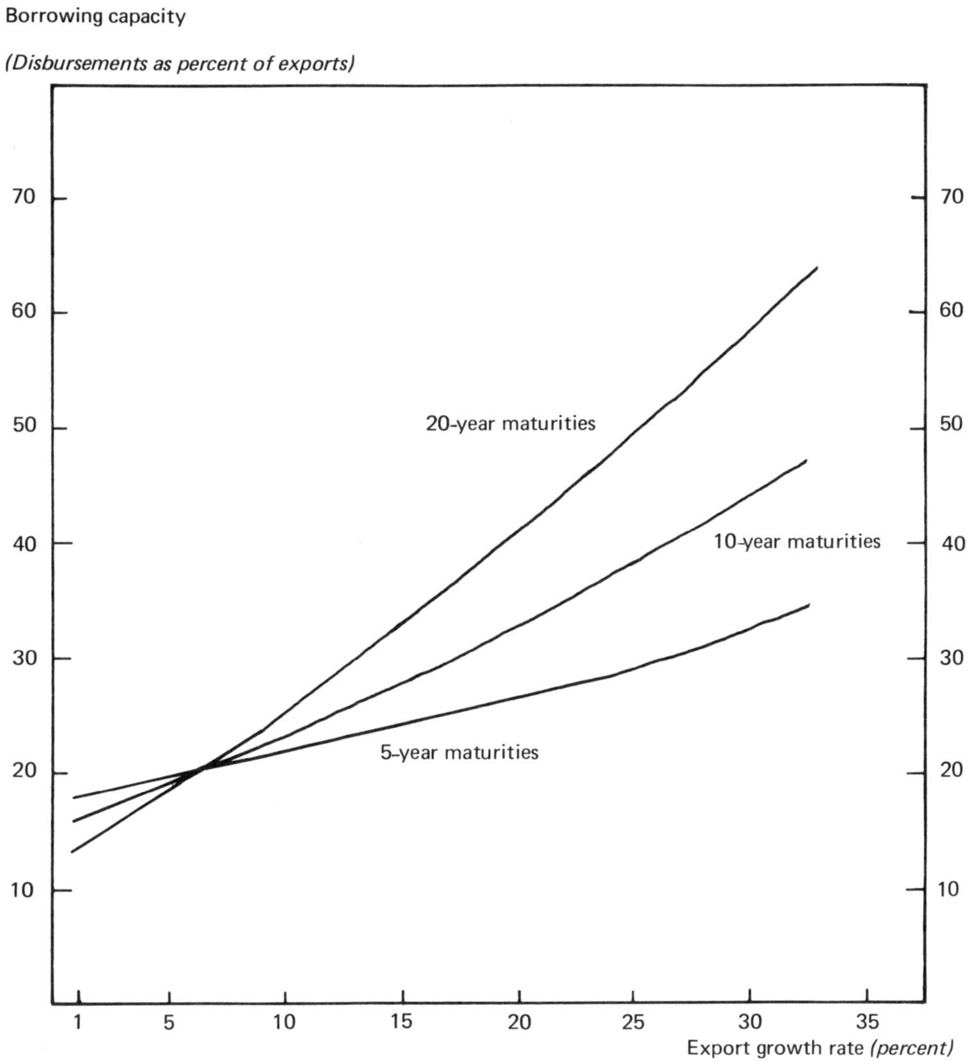

Source: Table 6-2.

Figure 6-1. Export Growth and Borrowing Capacity.

Optimal Debt

Other things being equal, borrowing capacity increases in line with the accepted debt-service ratio. Other things are not equal, however. As a country expands its borrowings beyond whatever limited access to official financing

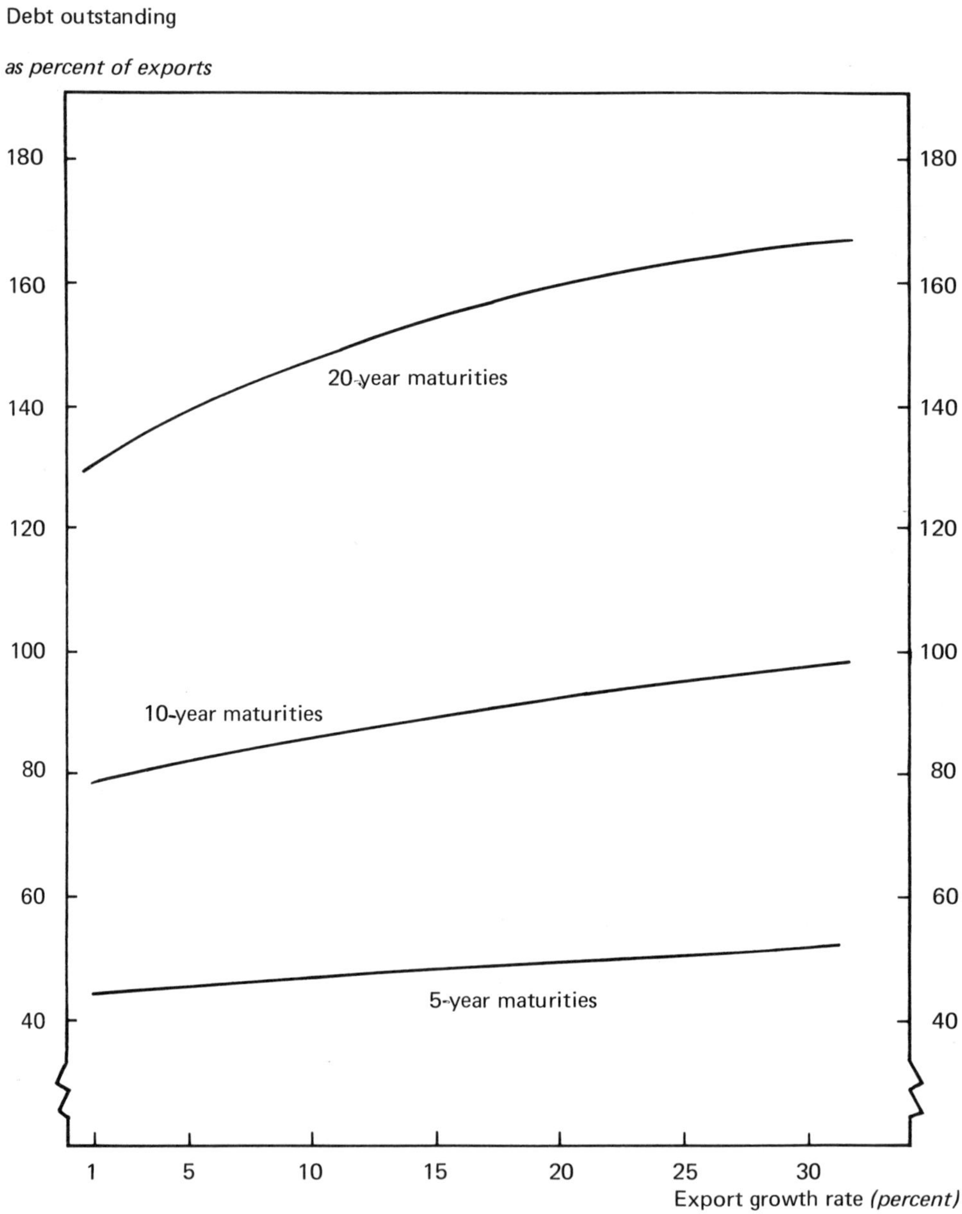

Source: Table 6-2.

Figure 6-2. Export Growth and the Level of Debt.

it may have, its average terms deteriorate, and along with them its refinancing ratio. Because of this the increase in borrowing capacity is not proportionate to that of the debt-service ratio, and at some point the difference between the two ratios is maximum. At that point the country is securing the highest sustainable net transfer: this is the "Loser criterion."

Depending on the shape of the loan supply curve, however, the maximum net transfer may be reached only for a high refinancing ratio; while the highest possible, the net transfer would be only a small share of disbursements. This cannot leave the borrower undisturbed.

Foreign money is no free good. This is not a reference to interest charges, which are assumed to be rolled over; the reference is to a bundle of other costs which are diverse and effective. Such are the cost of project identification for project loans, the demands on the time and energy of officials in the borrowing country to negotiate the loans, and the strain of political submission to creditors. Obviously, there are benefits to the process; project evaluation, for example, is one of the most valuable forms of technical assistance. Indeed, it is not infrequently the local administration's own deficiencies which most restrain effective borrowing capacity. Yet these are costs, and they call for a commensurate benefit. The benefit is the net transfer of resources. It is justifiable therefore to expect the net transfer to amount to a stated minimum share of disbursements; failing that, the whole game would not be worth playing. Accordingly, the policy objectives are not only to achieve a net transfer, but also to achieve it under reasonable cost-benefit conditions. The optimal borrowing policy may involve the imposition of an additional constraint, bearing on the refinancing ratio: borrow all you can, so long as it is sustainable, provided, however, the refinancing ratio does not deteriorate beyond a given point. This is the Loser criterion with an additional constraint.

Optimality in that sense, and even more so in the sense of the unrestricted Loser criterion, is different in nature from optimality under the "critical interest rate" approach. That approach could be called "economic"; its emphasis is on national income. The borrowing-capacity approach, on the other hand, could be called "financial"; its emphasis is on disposable income. It ensures that foreign claims, as they are built up, are not divested from the recipient economy, but are continuously rolled over.

The two approaches are not mutually inconsistent: an increase in interest rates, other things being equal, will reduce optimal borrowings under both approaches. In effect, they are complementary, and a fully rational policy would be one which satisfies both the critical-interest-rate condition and the Loser criterion, whichever is more restrictive. This would provide an economic rationale for a constrained Loser criterion.

In addition to the difference in the income concept, the two approaches are distinguished in that under the borrowing-capacity approach, as outlined here, no feedback effect of external borrowing on the growth of the recipient economy is allowed for, while consideration of this feedback is essential to the critical-interest-rate approach.

This, however, is not a substantive difference but only one which attaches to the treatment of the subject here. It would be a simple matter of analytical refinement to build up feedback effects of borrowing capacity on export performance through a parameter for rate of transformation of foreign resources into exports. It is felt, however, that ordinarily only a limited fraction of domestic investment plans has a direct bearing on export trends, so that the adjustment of the investment program to various borrowing assumptions need not bear on these trends. The practical implication is to develop a realistic estimate of the export growth rate and to ensure that domestic investment is properly geared to attain it. Where, by exception, external resources can make the difference for exports, alternative solutions will, of course, need to be explored.

Country Risk Analysis

An important application of the determination of borrowing capacity is in the evaluation of a country's borrowing policy.

A country is not simply "creditworthy" or not. A given policy is creditworthy in a given environment; a change in policy or a change in the environment may very rapidly alter the picture. For that reason, creditworthiness rating must always be a comprehensive undertaking, allowing, for example, for the consideration of such indirectly related but highly relevant variables as the borrower's administrative capacity to handle and coordinate its external debts.

As part of this broad process, however, a synthetic measure of the degree of realism of the borrower's policies can be useful. It is suggested that the above definition of borrowing capacity is helpful in this respect. A basic requirement which must be satisfied by borrowing policies is that they be sustainable. What needs to be assessed therefore is not the present level of debt as it now stands as a result of previous policies but its future level as it will obtain from current policies. The focus should be on those policies rather than on current debt only.

The suggested routine therefore is quite simple: it reverses the definition of borrowing capacity. This has been defined as the limit to the sustainable borrowings-to-exports ratio consistent with a ceiling on the debt-service ratio. The routine evaluates the debt-service ratio implicit in the borrowing policy under evaluation.

The borrowing policy can be identified through the contemplated volume of disbursements, their growth rate, and their terms.

The terms and volume can be known from declarations of intent or from recent behavior. In a number of cases, medium-term development plans delineate the economy's borrowing requirements. In other cases, recent commitments data can be used, although care must be exercised to determine whether these data truly reflect policy: because of administrative or other constraints, there may be a notable short-term variability of commitments. In periods of falling spreads or market interest rates, for example, larger borrowings may be arranged, simply for the purpose of refinancing former, costlier loans before maturity. Some medium-term forecasting of investment and the balance of payments will usually be helpful in assessing underlying trends. The growth rate of disbursements may well be taken to be the anticipated long-term exports growth rate. That particular assumption eliminates any disequilibrium in respect of the growth of debt, and the routine accordingly concentrates on adequacy of terms and volume, given an export performance. In cases of low initial indebtedness, it is true, the borrower enjoys some leeway in the relative growth of debt and exports; this, however, can be allowed for in a simple extension of the exercise.

With these elements in hand, the substance of the exercise is to compute the steady-state or "forward" debt-service ratio involved in the contemplated policy. This is not a forecast, but the derivation of logical implications of the policy, given its environment. It is really a further specification of that policy. Initial debt is disregarded as irrelevant because current policy rather than current debt determines the trend in indebtedness. The evaluation is therefore quite simple: if the forward ratio is felt to be excessive, either from reference to a given norm or by comparison to the current ratio, then that current policy is not sustainable, and conversely.

Thus defined, the forward debt-service ratio is altogether very different from the standard current ratio. The latter measures current debt as entailed by past policies; the former describes the trend in debt service as brought about by current policies. The latter accounts for only the level of debt; the former also accounts for the growth rate of exports and disbursements and for the terms. As an illustration, the forward debt-service ratio has been computed for the eight nonoil "debt heavyweights" of chapter 2, in order to compare policies followed some time before 1970 to those implemented in the early 1970s.

In each case the policies were identified with recent behavior: it was assumed that average commitment levels and terms over the four years from 1970 to 1974, respectively, would be sustained over extended periods, with commitments growing in line with trend exports for the period (table 6-3).

Under this approach, the policies followed by the sample countries have changed markedly over the turn of the decade. All countries have a very large reliance on foreign capital: new commitments amount to over 30 percent of exports in most cases, and much more for some countries. That reliance was somewhat reduced in 1974 compared to 1970, with Egypt and Mexico as exceptions in this regard. Terms, on the other hand, have frequently deteriorated, but not in a systematic way; those of India, for instance, have improved. The real change, however, is in the growth rate of

Table 6-3
Eight Developing Countries: Forward Debt-Service Ratios, 1970 and 1974
(percent)

		Commitments Ratio[a]	*Interest Rate*	*Maturities (Years)*	*Growth Rate of Exports*[b]	*Debt-Service Ratio Observed*[a]	*Debt-Service Ratio Forward*
Argentina	1970	27.8	6.0	11.6	4.2	25.0	30.3
	1974	29.1	7.3	10.1	10.2	18.3	26.0
Brazil	1970	33.2	5.5	15.2	11.3	15.2	24.3
	1974	35.7	7.3	13.8	30.0	14.1	15.1
Egypt	1970	19.8	3.5	10.1	7.6	21.8	16.6
	1974	33.8	4.3	18.7	19.0	21.4	14.8
India	1970	36.4	2.3	33.4	3.0	20.5	33.3
	1974	32.8	1.8	37.5	14.2	19.9	9.5
Korea	1970	58.0	4.6	14.6	35.2	12.7	17.3
	1974	32.4	6.4	16.8	38.5	12.3	9.6
Mexico	1970	32.4	7.2	9.9	7.4	25.3	32.2
	1974	41.9	8.7	12.0	17.1	21.3	30.0
Pakistan	1970	80.4	2.9	28.1	4.7	20.3	66.7
	1974	66.5	2.9	23.9	10.2	21.6	36.7
Turkey	1970	47.2	3.2	22.3	7.3	15.3	33.8
	1974	17.9	4.3	23.8	35.9	8.2	4.0

Sources: Data from World Bank, "World Debt Tables, 1976," vol. 2; International Monetary Fund, *International Financial Statistics,* August 1976, and estimates; computed from appendix A.

[a]1967-1970 or 1971-1974 average as percentage of average exports of goods and services for the same period.

[b]1965-1970 or 1969-1974 trend growth rate for exports of goods and services.

exports and accordingly in the assumed growth of disbursements. For all countries that rate strongly increased, even trebled in some cases. Only in Korea was the acceleration just modest; but then the going rate was impressive.

Accordingly, the underlying trends show considerable improvement. With the exception of Egypt, the comparison of the 1970 observed and forward ratios indicates that conditions prevailing at the end of the 1960s were leading to a deterioration of the debt-service ratios. As conditions changed, these prospects did not materialize, and all countries have experienced a decline in the debt-service ratio between 1970 and 1974. Moreover, the trend has been reversed: except for Mexico and Pakistan, the forward 1974 ratio is lower than the observed ratio. Finally, reflecting the accelerating export growth as well as a lower reliance on debt, the forward debt-service ratio shows considerable improvement in all cases.

It is thus possible in this fashion (although specific applications require a more cautious identification of policies) to provide a simple summary of the debt accumulation process. At the same time, the results display a high sensitivity to changing assumptions. The above example shows that borrowing conditions were better in 1974 than in 1970: but the improvement is due to stronger export growth and will last only if that growth rate continues.

Debt and Inflation

The definition of borrowing capacity can also be used to analyze the influence of various "external" factors. One of these is the variability of export earnings, due notably to the fluctuations in world prices for primary commodities; another is the trend of world inflation.

The variability of export earnings has a negative impact on borrowing capacity; the extent of that adverse effect depends on the magnitude of the possible cumulative fluctuations and on the decisionmaker's risk aversion. Faced with uncertain export prospects, the policymaker needs to make allowance for compensatory financing and/or shortfalls in export earnings, which would drive up the effective debt-service ratio. In the case of nonfluctuating exports, all that needs to be determined is maximum exposure, for example, a ceiling on the debt-service ratio. In the case of fluctuating exports, the ceiling cannot be defined as a stated figure, but as a probabilistic schedule. This is because exports are random, as well as debt service—at least insofar as the country relies on compensatory financing to offset the export fluctuations. The actual debt-service ratio at some future time can accordingly be thought of as comprising a trend component plus a random element. The trend component relates debt service on development borrowings to trend exports, while the random element accounts for debt service on compensatory financing and for deviations of exports from trend. The decisionmaker must then express his preferences in the form of acceptable probabilities for specified debt-service ratios. Unless he is a risk lover, the certainty-equivalent to that schedule will be a lower figure than the corresponding trend component of the debt-service ratio. This can be seen intuitively. Because of export fluctuations, the country must set aside some portion of exports as reserves, so that as a matter of policy not all export earnings are freely usable. The liquidity constraints of (trend) debt-service payments are therefore more sensitive in the case of export fluctuations, as the base for these payments is reduced by the need to accumulate reserves. In short, the existence of export fluctuations means that additional "room for maneuver" must be arranged, compared to the case of export stability; and to secure that additional leeway, additional restraint is in order.

Changes in the world inflation rate, if uncertain, will have the same effect as export variability—they will be a cause of export variability. The proper question about inflation, then, is not about the changes in its rate, but about its trend: Does inflation boost borrowing capacity in the long run?

A case for inflation could seemingly be constructed on the basis of experience in the early 1970s. The borrowing capacity of developing countries was obviously supported by the high nominal growth rate for their exports. On closer inspection, however, this may only have been transient, medium-run circumstance. The inflationary burst of the period was fueled by a monetary expansion which kept nominal interest rates relatively low, so that real interest rates fell. Accordingly, while nominal interest rates lagged behind, the nominal growth rate of exports and the spread between the two, which is an essential variable in the process, were strongly increased.

In the long run, however, two adjustments will cancel this transient effect: real interest rates will catch up as nominal interest rates adjust upward to the rate of inflation, and average maturities will shrink because higher inflation rates are associated with a greater uncertainty. The two effects will cancel the initial beneficial effects of unanticipated inflation on borrowing capacity.

Altogether inflation as such is unlikely to be favorable to borrowing capacity in the long run, although it may have been a transitory expedient to facilitate adjustment in the early 1970s.

As a qualification of that conclusion, however, the transition to lower rates of inflation may create some difficulties. This is because disbursements will follow the trends of current inflation, while debt service arising out of past disbursements will follow those of past inflation. As inflation abates, the differing trends of disbursements and debt service may squeeze out the net transfer.

Part IV
The Stake

As inflation exacerbated and oil prices soared, significant stress was experienced in the world trade and payments system. Large deficits, or sudden shortfalls, showed up in a number of countries, while oil producers registered unprecedented surpluses.

Under the circumstances, debt accumulation by developing countries acted as a powerful shock absorber. It could do so because inflation accelerated their export growth and their borrowing capacity as well. The logic of debt, however, is inflexible and could not accommodate a growth of borrowing requirements in excess of the increase in borrowing capacity.

Borrowing capacity mostly depends on activity in industrial countries, which is essential to the exports of developing countries. It is also affected by the availability of official loans.

Borrowing requirements are those imposed to roll over the swelling debt-service payments and those needed to cover the current account deficit and the formation of reserves. The current account deficit is also a function of activity in industrial countries.

Requirements and capacity thus both depend on the upturn in activity in industrial countries. If activity picks up strongly, the exports of developing countries will increase rapidly, and the oil deficit will be shared more evenly. Should it slow down, then a diminished borrowing capacity will be hard put to face up to magnified borrowing requirements.

Even under the most favorable conditions, some strains will be felt. The net transfer of resources through debt operations will become minimal, at least for the "commercial" borrowers, while their debt will remain high and its liquidity short. It is necessary to prepare for a deceleration of debt and to take further measures to ensure its stability. Among these, a continual expansion of official lending is desirable. Basically, however, trade performance is crucial. The growth of international trade is a prerequisite for a sustainable debt. The reverse, however, is also true. In the absence of a sustained demand from nonoil developing countries, activity in industrial countries will not show a marked advance; and demand from developing countries will not be sustained unless their debt is bearable. It is a clockwork: debt and international trade will flourish together or will flounder together.

7 A New Relationship

In the original design of the 1960s, the accumulation of debt was largely related to development assistance. This relation was evidenced in a large share of official flows in total net lending as well as in the dominant preoccupations of the period. Concern with the rising debt of developing countries arose in large part from its possible adverse implications for increased flows of external assistance, rather than from its potential threats for world trade and payments. And the determination of the second United Nations' development decade to increase official development assistance to 0.7 percent of GNP of developed countries was more than wishful thinking—it was the identification of a desirable trend.

Things have changed. While still a vehicle for a transfer of resources, the accumulation of debt now fulfills a new range of functions. In many middle-income countries, its net contribution to domestic investment is small or marginal, and its basic function lies in the intermediation of domestic savings. On a global scale, it acts as a buffer to facilitate the adjustment of world trade to the disturbances arising from world inflation and from the oil price increase. In many respects the debt of developing countries in the middle-income range is now similar in nature to that of the developed countries.

Recent Trends in Perspective

Debt developments in recent years have been supported by sustained economic growth in middle-income countries. Moreover, as noted in chapter 2, these countries have undergone extensive structural change. The share of manufacturing industry has much increased, in relation to both total output and exports, making those countries more vulnerable to protectionist pressures in industrial countries. The share of investment in GDP increased strongly and, with an average 26 percent in 1975, is now higher than that in industrial countries. More significantly, the savings ratio is high enough to sustain investment at high levels.

Structural and income differences between developed countries and the middle-income developing ones have thus been sharply reduced, and an inflow of net external resources is not essential to the pursuit of the process, although the conditions for a reversal of the net flow may not be met for a long time.

Building on this trend, a major result of the oil crisis is that economic stability in developed countries has become dependent on economic advances in the developing ones. The reverse, of course, is also true, but that has been known for a long time. The novel point is that dependence now works both ways, although it is perhaps not fully understood how far the process has now come.

A reason why this interdependence is not obvious, and an indication of the role of the oil crisis proper, is that trade among industrialized countries represents a major proportion of their total external trade as well as of world trade. This, however, was considerably changed because of the oil shock: in 1972, 31 percent of total exports of industrial countries (OECD countries, except for developing countries in Southern Europe) and 30 percent of their imports were in trade with nonindustrial areas; by 1975 these shares had increased to 39 and 38 percent respectively.[1] That is a 25 percent reduction in self-dependency. In addition, these global figures underestimate the reduction in self-dependency of industrial countries because they do not account for the structure of their trade with other regions. A large part of the imports of industrial countries from the rest of the world [about 55 percent, based on General Agreement on Tariffs and Trade (GATT) classifications][2] is made up of fuels, while most of their exports (over 80 percent, on the same basis) consists of manufactures. Nonoil developing countries, in absorbing increased amounts of the latter, have allowed the industrial countries to pay for the former: based again on GATT classifications, their imports from industrial countries increased by $34 billion from 1972 to 1975, making up for over one-third of the increased fuel imports of industrial countries over the period.

Debt and the Adjustment Process

Debt accumulation has not been alien to the growing commercial interdependence of developed and developing regions. It has been part of the international adjustment process, and in turn it imposes new constraints on that process.

The contribution of debt accumulation to trade stabilization in the mid-1970s can be seen from the way it helped offset the deflationary surge in world savings entailed by the oil price increase. A measure of that increase is the $37 billion additional trade surplus of oil producers in 1975, compared to 1973. Against this, debt accumulation by nonoil developing countries financed additional demand of $23.4 billion, that is, offset more than 60 percent of the increase in savings.[3]

This was not a plain accident: a very strong element of logical consistency was involved.

There prevails a worldwide necessary accommodation of current account balances for all country groups; the surplus of any given group is necessarily the deficit of its trading partners and conversely.

Matching the deficit of nonoil developing countries is therefore a combined surplus of the rest of the world. That surplus does as much for the deficit of the developing countries as the policies followed by these countries. The accumulation of debt, a corollary to that deficit, is therefore a global phenomenon. It enabled developing countries to postpone their adjustment, but the adjustment would have been less if the oil producers' surplus had been more fully offset by a deficit of the developed countries.

During a first period, 1974-1975, the combined reactions of developed countries led to a recession, whereas current account deficits in developing countries soared to unprecedented heights. These reactions were a result not simply of the oil price increase, but also of adjustment to "nonoil" deficits among industrial countries and more broadly of the fight against inflation. Whatever the case, the end result was a brutal shift of the current account balance of industrial countries from a $10 billion deficit in 1974 to a $19 billion surplus in 1975.[4] That turnabout was partly offset by a lower oil producers' surplus, but it also fell hard on other countries, raising their deficits while the recession was dampening their export growth.

The stabilizing influence of debt accumulation during that period is also apparent in the way it accumulated. Two-thirds of the total increase in debt from 1970 to 1975 and 75 percent of the increase in the debt of middle-income countries were in the form of private loans on market terms. Market loans flow out of market relationships: the driving force underlying their increase was obviously not aid in any significant sense of the word. It was not even development assistance in the wider sense of accelerating growth, but market adjustment to new conditions.

As the initial oil surpluses materialized in 1974, before oil countries had time to devise a diversified investment strategy, the surpluses were to a large extent placed on term deposits with a few major international banks. Shortly thereafter, the demand for credit in industrial countries began to weaken because of the recession, while it increased in developing countries because of a delayed adjustment to increased import costs and a weaker demand for their exports. The absorption of the oil surplus by developing countries through the intermediation of the banks was the financial counterpart of their role in mitigating the trade recession of 1975.[5]

Debt accumulation at such a rate, however, is only a shock absorber, not a durably reliable instrument. This was made clear in a second period, 1976 to 1977, as the financial markets ceased to be net suppliers of resources to developing countries.

One factor underlying this development is the change in the pattern of medium-term lending by the banks: disbursements do not keep abreast of the surge of debt-service payments, which means that an increasing share of new loans simply rolls over the old ones. This result of the relatively hard terms of private loans did not materialize in 1973-1976 because disbursements were growing so rapidly in the period. It is, however, unreasonable to expect them to proceed at that rate in the medium term, and already the fall of the net transfer is observable. The net flow of medium-term bank loans to nonoil developing countries, as recorded in the International Monetary Fund's 1978 annual report, has been reduced from $10.6 billion in 1976 to $9.4 billion in 1977. Allowing for an estimate of interest payments, this may amount to a reduction in the net transfer of over 25 percent, although gross flows have kept increasing.

Moreover, owing to the improved structure of regional balances of payments and to the rising U.S. deficit, international reserves of developing countries have been swelling, and the increase in their deposits with private banks has been in excess of their net new borrowings from the market. Along with geographic intermediation, the banks are now intermediating terms on behalf of developing countries; and external financing has evolved into a balanced intermediation process involving only a limited net transfer. The net external claims of banks reporting to the Bank for International Settlements on nonoil developing countries thus increased by only $3.5 billion from 1975 to 1977, while gross claims were growing by $29.2 billion. Indeed, in all regions except Latin America, net claims were reduced during that period, and even for Latin America their $10.9 billion increase was only half of the $20.5 billion increase in gross claims. Even in a famed trouble case such as Zaire, the banks' assets increased by $50 million during this period, while their liabilities were increasing by $60 million.

The Bank for International Settlements statistics, of course, cover all maturities, and the share of medium-term activity is greater for bank claims than for their liabilities. On a medium-term basis, therefore, the picture would be different, but that is precisely the relevant point: the banks are financing medium-term credit to developing countries out of these countries' own short-term deposits.

In retrospect, the growth of debt in 1973-1976 and the large net transfer which it made possible appear as a once-over operation. Under the terms of private lending, there is no realistic growth rate of disbursements that will keep debt service much below disbursements. Except for the low-income countries, who need official lending, the accumulation of debt will now serve the primary functions of intermediating terms for each country and of assisting in the process of international adjustment, rather than of providing real resources for development.

The emergence of this new situation transforms the politics of debt management but leaves the mechanics unchanged. Debt management will not, and except for low-income countries should not, yield substantial net transfers in the future. Sustained borrowing should, however, be undertaken, both to provide intermediation for the borrower's own savings and to roll over the liabilies accumulated in the past. While the benefits from the process may seem to be diminished because the net transfer vanishes, its costs, managerial and psychological, will fortunately also be lessened because of the generalization of untied balance-of-payments loans and growing acceptance of debt as a fact of life.

8 Walking the Tightrope

Important steps toward sustainable forms of external indebtedness have been taken in 1976-1977. Progress in the international adjustment of balances of payments has allowed for a lower rate of growth of external debt, practical solutions have been found in the problem cases, and greater recognition of the specific needs of the low-income countries has prevailed—with very little practical effect, however.

Those favorable developments are fortunate because the debt of middle-income countries is and will remain huge, and rather unstable. While the external financing of these countries is in many respects comparable to that of industrial countries, the orders of magnitude are disproportionate. With a large share of that overhang coming up for renewal each year, the scope for disruptions is very real.

Disruptions, if serious, could undo what the accumulation of debt achieved: they could destabilize the world economy, which would create a serious adjustment problem. The effects would spread cumulatively through trade, as developing countries would be forced into restrictive economic policies, and through the financial structure of industrial countries.

To handle this risk requires action on three points. First, and most important, trade must expand. The growth of export earnings is the basic condition for a smooth rollover; high export earnings are also essential for a continuing structural change in developing countries. Second, reliance on debt must be lessened. New borrowings should be curtailed to a level as low as possible in order to limit the long-term increase in the debt-service ratio or, if possible, to reduce that ratio. A greater inflow of official loans would be helpful in this respect, provided it is not achieved at the expense of the developmental needs of low-income countries. Third, mutual confidence must be built up, with the backing of national supervising agencies, if necessary. Together these measures can stabilize the debt of developing countries. All three are necessary; trade expansion is the most indispensible.

IBRD Projections

There are a number of possible projections of the trends of external debt of developing countries into the next decade, depending notably on assumptions made about the growth rate and terms of official lending. One of these projections, of evident interest, is that of the IBRD's 1978 World Development Report (table 8-1). This projection involves a debt outstanding of $650 billion and annual disbursements of $208 billion by 1985, while the debt-service ratio would soar to over 19 percent on the average, that is, nearly twice the 1975 figure.

The IBRD projections, which explore one of several possible futures and are not intended as a forecast, are predicated on several explicit assumptions: a 4.2 percent real GDP growth in industrial countries, allowing for a 6.3 percent volume increase in exports of developing countries; a 7 percent annual price increase; and average maturities of five years on private loans. The trends which they outline confirm that the role of debt is changing. For low-income countries, because external financing would be entirely in the form of official loans, debt service would remain low and would absorb only about 40 percent of disbursements. For middle-income countries, on the other hand, there would be a drastic change, for debt service would rise not only in relation to exports, but also relative to disbursements: it would absorb nearly three-quarters of disbursements in 1985, as against 55 percent in 1975. The net transfer would fall accordingly. The extent of its relative decline is, in fact, underestimated in table 8-1. First, the projections in that table are based on an average 6.2 percent interest rate on debt of middle-income countries. This is an unrealistic assumption, in view of the 7 percent price increase hypothesis; in the long run, real interest rates must be restored, or else there will be no sustained recovery of the real economy.

Table 8-1
Selected IBRD Projections for 1985
(billions of U.S. dollars and percent)

	Low-Income Countries		*Middle-Income Countries*		*Total*	
	1975	*1985*	*1975*	*1985*	*1975*	*1985*
Debt outstanding	34.2	112.5	127.9	536.1	162.1	648.6
Official sources	(27.0)	(104.0)	(44.4)	(186.3)	(71.4)	(290.3)
Private sources	(7.2)	(8.5)	(83.5)	(349.8)	(90.7)	(358.3)
Disbursements	8.5	22.1	40.1	185.8	49.0	208.0
Amortization payments	1.5	5.1	14.3	102.8	15.8	107.9
Interest payments	0.8	3.6	7.6	33.7	8.4	37.3
Total debt service	2.3	8.7	21.9	136.5	24.2	145.2
Exports[a]	20.5	73.9	185.5	672.2	206.0	746.0
Debt service ratio (percent)	11.2	11.8	11.8	20.3	11.7	19.5

Source: Based on data from World Bank, *World Development Report*, Washington, 1978, tables 29 and 30; and Robert S. McNamara, *Address to the Board of Governors*, Washington, IBRD, 1978, appendix tables 1 and 2.

[a]Goods and nonfactor services.

Second, because of the rising debt-service ratio, there would be a need for accumulating reserves at a pace which would absorb half the projected net transfer of resources. The remainder therefore would be very small indeed and would contribute to a declining share of domestic investment. In effect, under these projections, middle-income developing countries would be providing in the form of debt service and placement of reserves most of the finance required to fund their borrowings.

Favorable Factors

For the low-income countries, the projection calls for a continuation of the prevalent situation: out of necessity, concessional financing should be made available to achieve a net transfer of resources.

In the case of middle-income countries, a new situation is outlined, one in which the advantage of securing a lower net transfer may have to be weighed against the disruptions of higher disbursements and debt service. On current cost-benefit standards, the 1985 projection would not seem to be viable. There are indications, however, of a growing willingness to accept this new situation.

The possibility of political defaults first has been tested and rejected in 1976-1977. The test was rather strong because it was comprehensive, involving the multilateral diplomatic experiment of the Geneva discussions and the real-life cases of Zaire, Argentina, Peru, and Turkey. A major import of the March 1978 Geneva agreement to renegotiate the debts of the low-income countries is its implication *not* to renegotiate the commercial debt of middle-income countries. Similarly, in the problem cases, the news also was in the form of nonevents: defaults were avoided and situations, however precarious, were frozen. A pattern has been established, that of refinancing, rather than of calling a formal default.

Meanwhile, the dedramatization of debt as a commercial relationship facilitates the political acceptability of higher debt levels. The growing role of balance-of-payments loans by private banks is instrumental in this respect, because these loans escape many of the problems of geographic or project tying which make other lending burdensome. Higher debt-service ratios can be tolerated because their disruptive effects are lessened. Altogether, the possibility of a global default on political-strategic grounds has become an unlikely prospect.

A second important ground for optimism is that international adjustment has now advanced to a point where a massive net transfer of resources to middle-income countries is no longer required. As noted, the initial reaction of industrial countries to inflation and the oil price increase resulted in a deflationary situation, which the accumulation of debt helped mitigate.

By contrast, the swelling U.S. deficit of 1976-1978 and the increased imports of oil countries have resulted in a more satisfactory current account structure in 1977. The absurd surplus of industrial countries vanished, while that of oil exporters was reduced, so that the deficit of nonoil developing countries was curtailed both in absolute terms and, even more so, relative to exports. Indeed, the IMF found that, allowing for changes in prices and activity, the 1977 current account deficit of nonoil developing countries other than those in Southern Europe was not greater than in 1967-1972.[1]

Finally, the inflation of recent years has helped to erase a sizable part of the debt. As noted in chapter 1, the debt outstanding is currently not greater relative to exports than before the oil crisis.[2]

On "objective" and "psychopolitical" grounds, there is accordingly some reason to consider that debt prospects as outlined in table 8-1 are viable, although they may not be desirable.

Winds from the Cold

There is a big difference between the debt of developing countries and that of industrialized countries: it is one of dimension. The debt of developing countries is incomparably larger than that of developed countries. While the developing countries are stepping into external financial intermediation on much the same basis as industrial countries, they are doing so on a vastly larger scale. To take a crude yardstick, compare the external liabilities to banks of major industrial countries, relative to their exports of goods and services, and those of major developing borrowers, in 1975: the differences are impressive. First, in terms of debt outstanding, Bank for International Settlements data indicate that the external claims of reporting banks (including interbank balances) on the United States as of the end of 1975 were 21 percent of the U.S. exports of goods and services. That ratio was 47 percent in the case of Japan, 86 percent for the United Kingdom, 33 percent for France, and 28 percent for Germany. This is a fairly open range of ratios, admittedly, but one outside which many developing countries clearly fall: 217 percent for Mexico, 149 percent for Brazil, and 128 percent for Peru, for example, although the ratio was only 56 percent for Korea and 37 percent for Spain.

Taken in terms of flows, the difference is even larger. World Bank compilations indicate that Eurocredits received and issues of international and foreign bonds in 1975 amounted to 0.7 percent of U.S. exports of goods and services, a share rising to 2.9 percent in the case of Japan, 2.0 percent for the United Kingdom, 3.2 percent for France, 0.2 percent for Germany, but 39 percent for Mexico, 22 percent for Brazil, 24 percent for Peru, 5.5 percent for Korea, and 7.9 percent for Spain. The difference is so large that it entails a question of substance, not just degree.

A second major original characteristic of the debt of middle-income developing countries is that debt service will keep increasing strongly, to the point of raising some serious adjustment problems.

Under the previously mentioned set of World Bank assumptions, the debt-service ratio of middle-income developing countries would reach 20 percent in 1985. This is a 9-point increase in ten years. To give some perspective, the additional oil bill of industrial countries in 1974 was 8 percent of their exports of goods and services of that year. Of course, the two magnitudes are not fully comparable: the latter increase was abrupt, while the former would be evened out over ten years. The oil price increase had direct implications for the savings-investment balance and disrupted the cost structure of production inputs, which debt service needs not do; the oil shock came on a background of soaring inflation, while inflation is now hopefully coming under control. Still, the far-reaching effects of the oil price increase are an indication that adjustments of that magnitude are not all too easy to manage.

Finally, the debt of developing countries, no matter how dedramatized, remains inordinately sensitive to developments affecting the borrowing capacity of these countries. Already 17 percent of debt outstanding has to be rolled over each year. If the projections in table 8-1 materialize, debt service will rise to 25 percent of debt outstanding, and the size of debt and of debt flows would still increase relative to world trade. Snow is piling up for an avalanche.

On the supply side, this situation is a challenge to the international banking system. In most industrial countries, monetary targets currently provide for a 7 to 12 percent annual increase in domestic credit. Compared to this, the debt of middle-income countries to private creditors is expected to grow at about 18 percent per year, which means that the banks' exposure to thse countries will increase. There should not be a shortage of loanable funds, however, because developing countries can be expected to provide most of the finance needed in the form of debt service and placements of resources, much as they have done in 1976-1977. The potential problems from increased exposure lie in the stability of the system rather than in the overall availability of funds. With a high proportion of debt maturing each year, individual borrowers are faced with a greater uncertainty about the willingness of banks to keep increasing their nominal exposure, just as the banks are faced with a risk that part of their assets could be temporarily illiquid because of adverse developments in some borrowing countries. This risk, for both borrowers and lenders, is increased because of the large degree of concentration of debt. The banks' exposure to Brazil and Mexico alone is greater than their total exposure to Eastern European countries, including the Soviet Union. A debt management problem with a single large borrower or, even more so, a change in policy by a single large bank, resulting in a deteriorating "investment climate," could result in widespread difficulties.

The recent trend to low spreads on the market does little to help in this respect. This trend has obvious positive aspects, because of its direct cost implications for the borrower and because it is a result of an enlarged access to financial markets. There is, however, an insurance component in these spreads which must be maintained, or even increased, especially for the smaller banks. Unless this is done, the smaller banks may lack the nerve and resources to withstand local difficulties and may tend to overreact.

On the demand side, borrowers may find that the balance of costs and benefits becomes unsatisfactory. It is one thing to get a 10 percent addition to your exports out of a 22 percent disbursements ratio; it is another to get an 8 or maybe a 6 percent addition out of a 30 percent ratio. Willingness as such is not at stake, but the pressure of facts, the potential volatility of supply, and the increased need to avoid bunching problems will increase the demands of having to negotiate such large amounts of loans, and debt management will become more difficult. The scope for using compensatory financing in the case of export shortfalls may be reduced because of the short maturity structure of debt outstanding. The balance between interest payments and the net flow of resources will also look less favorable.

A number of things can go wrong; the debt of middle-income countries is simply not stable enough. There is little likelihood of a full-scale default, which would truly jeopardize the financial system, although the accumulation of illiquid claims may grow uncomfortably large. But there is a distinct possibility that the addition of payments difficulties here and there may in the end significantly dampen the growth in world trade. The countries directly faced with payments difficulties would have to enforce restrictive demand policies, resulting in reduced imports from industrial countries; the industrial countries, in turn, may experience dissatisfaction with the change in their current account, and so on. The process can spread faster if creditors lose their confidence or lack the discipline required to resist the temptation of reducing their exposure. In short, while debt has mitigated the 1975 depression, it can do little now to hasten the pace of recovery and may well come as an obstacle in its way.

The seriousness of this potential threat should not be underestimated. The projections in table 8-1 are viable, but they are only viable because exports are projected to grow at a 13.7 percent annual rate, which is markedly higher than in the 1960s.

The impact of that assumption and its significance are worth stressing. The assumption is based on a 7 percent inflation rate and a 6.3 percent volume increase. The latter is predicated on a 4.2 percent real GDP growth in industrial countries, and the link is very strong. A 0.5 percent difference in the rate of growth of developed economies results in a 1 percent difference in the rate of growth of export volume of developing countries. If industrial countries manage only a 3.7 percent real growth until 1985—possibly because debt difficulties would hamper the implementation of expansionary policies—then exports of middle-income countries will be $606 billion instead of $672 billion in 1985, and the debt-service ratio will be 22.5 percent instead of 20 percent. On the other hand, a faster growth of industrial countries, say at a rate of 4.7 percent would allow exports of developing countries to increase to $740 billion and their debt-service ratio to drop to 18.5 percent. The difference between these figures must be considered very large, because they are average figures. As noted in chapter 3, the distributions of individual country ratios is rather skewed. A 4 percent difference in the average ratio really implies a much larger difference in the ratio for the "lead" group, or a large difference in the number of countries with ratios in excess of, say, 25 percent.

A small variation in the real growth rate of industrial countries would therefore result in large differences for the viability of the process.

Little comfort is to be drawn from the thought that a lower-than-projected growth performance would be associated with a higher rate of inflation. For one thing, this might not even work, since higher inflation along with lower activity levels may result in deteriorating terms of trade. Inflation does not safeguard the exports of developing countries. For another, while some inflation will be unavoidable yet for a few years, it is not desirable to build a mechanism which can operate only in an inflationary environment. Already in a number of countries, borrowing policy is framed on the assumption of inflationary export growth, resulting in inflated evaluations of borrowing capacity. The projection in table 8-1 is an extension of that procedure. If inflation does recede to 5 percent in 1980-1981, still a high figure, with real exports still growing at 6.3 percent annually, the debt-service ratio will again rise to 22.5 percent, and extensive difficulties are much more likely.

Policies

The growth of debt must decelerate more rapidly than projected in table 8-1. Unless it does, the possibility of extensive difficulties, resulting in a curtailment of real growth, and sustained inflation is significant. It does not pay to take that risk.

As indicated, an additional growth of 0.5 percent for the industrial economies would allow exports of developing countries to increase by an additional 1 percent. By 1985, this would result in a 10 percent addition to the volume of their exports. Even that figure underestimates the importance of the issue. Trade in manufactures is expected to be the most dynamic element of exports of developing countries. Its expansion is essential not only for its contribution to export growth, but also for the continuing structural change in these countries. Besides, a recovery in industrial countries is the only decisive way to stop the mounting pressures of protectionism and to press ahead with trade liberalization. It has been estimated that the complete dismantling of trade barriers could result in a $24 billion addition to exports of manufactures by developing countries in 1985.[3] This is a 3.5 percent addition to their total projected exports for that year. The difference between the favorable case and the unfavorable one is thus about 13 percent.

Against this, a drop of the growth rate of disbursements from a projected 16.5 percent to 12 percent, for example, would entail a reduction of the net transfer amounting to only 4 percent of exports by 1985, and the debt-service ratio would be cut to 15 percent. If that course of action facilitates a lower inflation rate, terms may improve and the reduction needs may not even be so large.

Altogether, developing countries have immense stakes in trade issues, and the scope for use of external resources does not measure up to the difference which a successful or unsuccessful outcome on trade could make. It does not pay to take a risk on trade to secure a little more debt.

A first requirement to keep debt within manageable limits is therefore to realize that middle-income countries have now reached a point on their debt cycle where a net transfer can, and should, be dispensed with. Given domestic savings ratios in excess of 20 percent, the projected net transfer under the above IBRD assumptions really does not materially change the growth prospects. Efficient utilization of capital, which depends on export opportunities for manufactures, is of greater importance; even where debt is concerned, it may be more useful to keep a margin of safety to accommodate compensatory financing of export fluctuations than to borrow to the hilt. One way to keep debt manageable is to borrow less.

Another requirement to keep debt under control is to ensure its stability. This should preferably be achieved by joint action on several points. Guidelines for handling commercial debt difficulties must be further elaborated, with a view to avoiding panic reactions. As a step toward this, some improvement in lending procedures is necessary, and greater restraint needs to be exercised by the banks and the regulatory agencies. Longer maturities would also help, in order to reduce the share of debt outstanding which needs to be rolled over each year. This can result from a higher share of official financing in total lending, which will obtain more easily if total flows increase less rapidly. Increased official lending can also help improve the stability of the system by providing compensatory financing on a broader scale, which would limit the global impact of local disruptions. Increased official lending should not, however, be directed to the achievement of substantially enlarged net transfers. The reason is that the middle-income countries can do without an additional net transfer, while whatever additional resources the collective shortsightedness of developed countries will make available are urgently needed by the low-income countries.

For these countries, debt will continue to be a significant source of investment and import capacity, amounting to about 12 percent of imports. Since these countries still record rather low savings ratios, these resources are of great importance. The amounts required are limited in absolute terms—a projected $10 billion net transfer in 1985, which is less than 0.1 percent of the projected GNP of industrial countries, but that would be 8 percent of investment in low-income areas.

Appendix A
The Mechanics of Debt

Notation

Let exports X proceed at a constant growth rate (a) from some initial value X_0:

$$X_t = X_0 e^{at}$$

We consider a series of disbursements (GF) growing at the same rate as exports from an initial value GF_0:

$$GF_t = GF_0 e^{at}$$

These loans are all repaid in T equal annuities. An interest rate i is charged on debt outstanding at the end of the previous period, D_{t-1}. We further define A_t, the flow of amortization payments in period t, and DS_t, the flow of debt-service payments in that period. Finally we write

g = disbursements ratio (GF/X)
p = debt-service ratio (DS/X)
d = debt ratio (D/X)
n = net transfer ratio [$GF - DS)/X$]
u = amortization ratio (A/X)

The value of all these ratios will be expressed as a function of T, i, and a, for the case where the process has been repeated for over T periods so that the value of all ratios has stabilized and has become independent of time.

Computations

The simplest approach starts with the amortization ratio. For $t > T$, we have

$$A_t = \frac{I}{T} \int_{t-T}^{t} GF_t$$

Therefore

$$A_t = \frac{KGF_t}{aT} \qquad \text{where } K = I - e^{-aT}$$

Dividing throughout by X_t yields

$$u = g\frac{K}{aT} \tag{A.1}$$

Debt outstanding at time t is the addition of debt outstanding at time T and of increments from T to t. D_T is the difference between cumulative disbursements and cumulative amortization payments:

$$D_T = \int_0^T GF_t - \frac{I}{T} \int_{\theta=0}^{T} \int_{t=0}^{\theta} GF_t$$

Increments in debt from T to t are equal to

$$D_t - D_t = (g - u) \int_T^t X_t$$

Substituting for u from (A.2) and rearranging give

$$d = \frac{g}{a}\left[1 - \frac{K}{aT}\right] \qquad \text{(A.2)}$$

and because by definition the debt-service ratio is

$$p = u + id \qquad \text{(A.3)}$$

all debt flows can be expressed in terms of i, a, and T.

Domar's Law

The necessary and sufficient condition for a positive net transfer, that is, to keep service charges below disbursements, is to maintain a growth rate of disbursements in excess of the interest rate, that is $a > i$.

A positive net transfer namely implies $n > 0$. Now, $n = g - p$. Substituting from (A.2) and (A.3) gives

$$n = g(1 - \frac{K}{aT})(1 - \frac{i}{a})$$

and

$$n = d(a - i) \text{ which is positive for } a > i. \qquad \text{(A.4)}$$

Refinancing Ratio

The *refinancing ratio* is defined as the share of debt service in disbursements, that is, p/g. Since $p/g = 1 - n/g$, substituting from (A.4) gives

$$p/g = 1 - d/g\,(a - i) = \frac{K}{aT}(1 - \frac{i}{a}) + \frac{i}{a} \qquad \text{(A.5)}$$

For given i and T, the ratio is a direct function of a. Thus the growth rate of disbursements is a major contributing factor to the refinancing ratio.

Forward Debt-Service Ratio

The *forward debt-service ratio* is the service ratio p arising when g, a, i, and T are maintained for over T periods.

From (A.5) that coefficient is

$$p = g\left[\frac{i}{a} + (1 - \frac{i}{a})\frac{K}{aT}\right] \qquad (A.6)$$

The forward ratio thus heavily depends on the export growth rate and the disbursements growth rate; it is lower, for given terms, when that rate is higher.

Borrowing Capacity

Borrowing capacity is defined as the highest sustainable disbursements ratio consistent with a given debt-service ratio. This amounts to computing the maximum for g, g^x, entailed by a constraint on p, p^x. Transforming (A.5) yields

$$g^x = p^x\left[\frac{i}{a} + (1 - \frac{i}{a})\frac{K}{aT}\right]^{-1} \qquad (A.7)$$

Borrowing capacity is therefore also a function of the exports' and disbursements' growth rate; and, other things being equal, borrowing capacity is larger when that rate is higher.

Appendix B
Statistical Material

Table B-1
Eighty-four Developing Countries: Creditor Composition of External Debt, 1972 and 1975
(billions of U.S. dollars and percent)

	1972		*1975*	
	$ Billion	*Percent*	*$ Billion*	*Percent*
Debt outstanding, including undisbursed	96.6	100.0	173.9	100.0
Official sources	67.2	69.6	107.3	61.7
Bilateral	(47.7)	(49.3)	(70.3)	(40.4)
Multilateral	(19.5)	(20.3)	(37.0)	(21.2)
Private sources	29.4	30.4	66.6	38.3
Suppliers	(12.7)	(13.2)	(18.7)	(10.8)
Financial markets	(15.7)	(16.2)	(46.7)	(26.9)
Other	(1.0)	(1.0)	(1.1)	(0.6)
Commitments	17.8	100.0	39.9	100.0
Official sources	10.8	57.8	18.4	46.1
Bilateral	(7.1)	(38.0)	(10.6)	(26.6)
Multilateral	(3.7)	(19.8)	(7.8)	(19.5)
Private sources	7.9	42.2	21.5	53.9
Suppliers	(2.2)	(11.7)	(5.1)	(12.8)
Financial markets	(5.7)	(30.5)	(16.4)	(41.1)

Source: World Bank, "World Debt Tables," mimeographed, Washington, 1977.
Note: Totals may not add, due to rounding.

Table B-2
Grant Element of Loan Commitments to Ninety-six Developing Countries, 1970, 1972, and 1976
(percent)

	1970	*1972*	*1976*
Official creditors	45	40	31
Bilateral	(51)	(42)	(34)
Multilateral	(33)	(34)	(27)
Private creditors	12	10	7
Suppliers	(15)	(11)	(8)
Financial Markets	(8)	(10)	(7)
Total loans	31	27	18
Total, loans and grants	37	33	22

Source: World Bank, "World Debt Tables," mimeographed, 1978; and *Annual Report*, 1978.

Table B-3
Comparative Debt Performance of Oil Producers and Other Developing Countries, 1972-1976
(cumulative growth rates in percent)

	Eighty-seven Nonoil Countries	*Nine Oil Producers*	*Ninety-six Developing Countries*
Debt outstanding disbursed	117.2	112.0	116.4
Disbursements	173.2	111.7	159.9
Debt Service	104.2	137.5	110.2

Source: Based on World Bank, "World Debt Tables," mimeographed, 1978.

Table B-4
Thirteen Renegotiation Cases: Debt and Debt Service
(percent)

Country	Year of Renegotiation (t)	Debt Ratio[a] (disbursed) t–1	t–4	Debt-Service Ratio[a] t–1	t–4
Argentina	1962	179.4	121.1	20.1	11 9
Brazil	1961	165.5	98.7	36.9	19.6
Chile	1965	147.3	110.8	21.1	24.6
Egypt	1966	146.6	95.3	12.6	2.7
Ghana	1966	141.3	38.4	33.7	6.2
India	1968	287.2	180.4	20.5	12.2
Peru	1968	69.1	35.7	10.7	5.8
Philippines	1970	32.2	26.5	4.0	6.8
Turkey	1959	100.9	84.2	21.5	n.a.
Turkey	1965	153.4	158.4	19.6	20.4
Uruguay	1965	65.1	73.5	6.0	5.9
Yugoslavia	1966	122.3	98.6	16.2	10.8
Yugoslavia	1970	42.8	62.0	8.5	11.9

Source: P. Dhonte, "Describing External Debt Situations: A Roll-Over Approach ' International Monetary Fund Staff Papers, March 1975.

[a]Percentage of exports of goods and services.

Table B-5

Thirteen Renegotiation Cases: Disbursements and Net Transfer

(percent)

Country	*Year of Renegotiation (t)*	*Disbursements as Percentage of Imports (t–1)*	*Net Transfer as Percentage of Imports*[a] *(t–4)*	*(t–1)*	*15-year Discounted Debt Service as Percentage of Debt Outstanding Including Undisbursed (t–1)*	*Debt Service as Percentage of Debt Outstanding (t–1)*
Argentina	1962	33.2	17.1	17.9	n.a.	13 3
Brazil	1961	45.5	16.7	14.9	n.a	26.6
Chile	1965	27.9	26.1	8.4	53.3	15.8
Egypt	1966	29.9	13.9	20.0	n.a.	11.0
Ghana	1966	34.0	21.5	13.2	73.4	29.5
India	1968	31.1	35.4	17.2	41.8	8.1
Peru	1968	16.5	12.0	6.9	62.4	18.4
Philippines	1970	6.9	5.0	3.4	75.7	14.9
Turkey	1959	n.a.	n.a.	n.a.	n.a.	n.a.
Turkey	1965	28.1	19.5	9.5	53.6	13.9
Uruguay	1965	6.5	4.9	n.a.	75.0	9.5
Yugoslavia	1966	49.2	25.2	33.0	70.3	18.7
Yugoslavia	1971	5.5	11.9	–1.9	74.5	20.1

Source: P. Dhonte, "Describing External Debt Situations: A Roll-Over Approach," International Monetary Fund Staff Papers, March 1975.

[a]Imports of goods and services.

Appendix C The Distribution of Debt

The distribution of external debts has been assessed on the basis of a sample of thirty-four large countries for which sufficient information was available. Such information comprised the volume and average terms (grant element) of commitments received from 1969 to 1971. These data were obtained from World Bank publications. The OECD's "Performance Compendium, 1974" was the source of a number of economic data such as the growth rate of real GNP, 1960 to 1970; income per capita in 1970 or 1971, depending on the country; the average savings ratio; and the incremental capital coefficient for 1965 to 1970. Exports data were obtained from the International Monetary Fund's "International Financial Statistics."

The sample involved the thirty-four following countries: Argentina, Brazil, Bolivia, Chile, Colombia, Ethiopia, Ghana, India, Indonesia, Iran, Iraq, Ivory Coast, Kenya, Korea, Malaysia, Mexico, Morocco, Nigeria, Pakistan, Peru, Philippines, Sri Lanka, Sudan, Syria, Taiwan, Tanzania, Thailand, Tunisia, Turkey, Uganda, Venezuela, Yugoslavia, Zaire, and Zambia.

The primary purpose of the study was to investigate the interdependence of volume and terms for new commitments and the relations between the volume of official commitments and that of private ones.

This required a specification of the equations for each of these variables. This was conducted by trial and error from a rather extensive list of explanatory variables, based on the approach outlined in the text. The specifications that gave the best fit with ordinary least squares were then adjusted with a two-stage least-squares routine.

The final specification is very simple. It relates the volume of official commitments (OFCX) and of private commitments (PCX), adjusted for the borrower's exports, and the grant elements of these commitments (GOFC and GPC, respectively) to the growth rate of GNP (YPCT), income per capita (IPC), the debt-service ratio (DSX), and the warranted growth rate (PE), that is, the ratio of the savings rate over the incremental capital coefficient. A dummy variable (CORR) was also introduced to allow for the exceptional terms of private commitments received by four countries.

The adjustments are as follows:

$$\underset{}{\mathrm{OFCX}} = \underset{4.43}{18.13} + \underset{4.30}{0.93\mathrm{DSX}} - \underset{3.81}{0.029\mathrm{IPC}} \qquad \overline{R^2} = 0.42 \tag{C.1}$$

$$\text{GOFC} = 83.49 - 0.038\text{IPC} - 4.16\text{YPCT} \qquad \text{(C.2)}$$

8.84 4.00 2.65 $\overline{R^2} = 0.43$

$$\text{PCX} = 11.89 + 0.64\text{DSX} + 2.22\text{YPCT} \qquad \text{(C.3)}$$

2.66 5.22 3.03 $\overline{R^2} = 0.53$

$$\text{GPC} = 16.57 + 0.28\text{PE} - 0.008\text{IPC} + 32.3\text{CORR} \qquad \text{(C.4)}$$

11.2 2.24 2.87 13.13 $\overline{R^2} = 0.87$

While the R^2 in equation (C.4) is rather high and the coefficients for PE and IPC are significant, this equation was felt to be misleading. Partial R^2 for PE and IPC are only 19 and 12 percent, respectively. Since PE is the warranted growth rate, a substitution of YPCT for PE would be expected to be significant; this, however, is not the case. Further, the sign of PE is surprising: why should countries with a higher growth potential obtain softer terms? Altogether, that relationship is likely to be spurious. IPC has the proper sign, but its partial correlation with GPC is weak. In short, GPC appears to be impervious to the influence of any of the variables used here.

Other variables have been tested and rejected. The savings ratio gave a proper coefficient, but its significance vanished when used jointly with IPC. Proper results were obtained with the growth rate of exports instead of that of GNP, but the fit was inferior.

With two-stage least squares, the following obtained:

$$\text{OFCX} = 8.62 + 0.91\text{DSX} - 0.022\text{IPC} + 0.16\text{GOFC} \qquad \text{(C.5)}$$

0.47 4.15 1.49 0.53 $\overline{R^2} = 0.41$

$$\text{GOFC} = 79.85 + 0.12\text{OFCX} - 0.036\text{IPC} - 4.21\text{YPCT}$$

6.03 0.40 3.15 2.56 $\overline{R^2} = 0.42$

$$\text{PCX} = 11.67 - 0.01\text{GPC} + 0.064\text{DSX} + 2.22\text{YPCT} \qquad \text{(C.6)}$$

2.26 0.09 5.05 3.00 $\overline{R^2} = 0.51$

$$\text{GPC} = 18.00 + 0.03\text{PCX} - 0.007\text{IPC} + 33.63\text{CORR}$$

12.01 0.25 2.24 13.04 $\overline{R^2} = 0.85$

$$\text{OFCX} = 17.44 + 1.12\text{DSX} - 0.03\text{IPC} - 0.33\text{PCX} \qquad \text{(C.7)}$$

4.01 2.60 2.86 0.53 $\overline{R^2} = 0.41$

$$\text{PCX} = 7.94 + 0.80\text{DSX} + 1.92\text{YPCT} - 0.22\text{OFCX}$$

1.53 4.83 2.54 1.42 $\overline{R^2} = 0.54$

$$\text{GOFC} = 83.61 - 0.039\text{IPC} - 4.27\text{YPCT} - 0.005\text{GPC} \qquad \text{(C.8)}$$

7.50 3.76 2.60 0.02 $\overline{R^2} = 0.41$

$$\text{GPC} = 13.48 - 0.006\text{IPC} + 32.45\text{CORR} + 0.27\text{PE} + 0.05\text{GOFC}$$
$$\quad\quad 2.09 \quad 1.07 \quad 12.92 \quad 2.15 \quad 0.50 \quad \overline{R^2} = 0.87$$

The coefficients for PCX, OFCX, GPC, and GOFC are not significant, an indication that the volume of private commitments is unrelated to that of public commitments and that grant elements for each source of loans do not depend on volume.

Fourteen of the thirty-four countries held meetings of their aid consortium or consultative group between 1969 and early 1971. A comparison of the average values of the dependent variables in the two groups shows that the countries with a consortium receive more official loans and on softer terms than other countries, while there is no significant difference in respect of private commitments. This result, however, mainly reflects differences in the values of the independent variables: when the above regressions are run for each subsample separately and comparing the results in covariance analysis, significant *F* ratios obtain only for OFCX. The existence of a consortium therefore only affects the distribution of the volume of official loans.

Appendix D
Statistical Sources

Loans to developing countries are fairly diverse in character. They can be sorted out on the basis of their financial terms, of various technical specifications, and of the nature of the lender.

Besides the specification of the currency, the financial characteristics of a loan mainly comprise its maturity and its interest rate.

The maturity of a loan cannot be simply expressed as a stated number of years. While the lapse of time between disbursements (which can themselves be staged in several installments) and final repayments can usually be unambiguously specified, mention must also be made of the amortization scheme and of the existence of a grace period prior to the first installment.

A typical case, to which the calculations of appendix A refer, is for an equal-annuity amortization schedule. That case obtains for many official loans and suppliers' credits; grace periods are frequently introduced, which have not been allowed for in appendix A.

Another significant case, relevant to many bank credits, involves one-shot amortization at the end of the lending period. Other formulas can be found in great number.

Interest rates can be fixed or variable. Variable interest rates are mostly encountered with bank credits, which frequently provide for a margin or "spread" ranging from 0.5 to 3 percent on top of the London interbank offer rate for the relevant currency for a specified maturity. The effective rate thus varies along with market conditions, usually at six-month intervals.

To summarize the terms, a synthetic measure has been devised under the name of "grant element." This is the difference between a loan's face value and the total of discounted charges on that loan, including interest, amortization, fees, and so forth. That difference is expressed as a percentage of the loan's face value. The grant element is positive when the discount rate is higher than the interest rate; it is larger, given a discount rate, when the interest rate is lower and when the maturity is longer. A high grant element indicates favorable terms, the limit being 100 percent in the case of grants. Standard practice, established by the Development Assistance Committee, is to use a 10 percent discount rate.

Lending on terms more favorable than those of the international capital markets is called concessional. The Development Assistance Committee designates as such all loans with a grant element of over 25 percent; however, it requires its members to achieve an overall 87 percent grant element for their official development assistance, including grants. A target of the United Nations Development Decade is to devote 0.7 percent of donor countries' GNP to official development assistance.

Next to the terms, several loan features have particular relevance.

First, a distinction is drawn between short- and medium-term loans, the latter group encompassing all loans with an initial maturity of over one year. The rationale for that distinction is that short-term loans are deemed to be the self-liquidating counterpart of trade relations, while long-term loans provide developmental financing.

Another distinction relates to the guarantees or insurances underwritten in support of the loan. On the borrower's side, the existence of a guarantee given by a public body serves to define "public" debts. On the lender's side, private lenders frequently secure additional securities in the lending country. These are offered by export credit insurance companies and benefit not only to straight suppliers' credits, but also to a number of bank facilities, for example, buyers' credits.

"Tying" is another important characteristic of a loan. Tying a loan is to impose specific restrictions on the use of its proceeds. The restrictions usually bear on geographic procurement (the goods must then originate from the lending country) or on project expenditure (the proceeds of the loan must then finance a specific venture).

Country tying is, in principle, a damaging practice since it bars the borrower from making full use of international competition to secure the best procurement conditions. It remains, however, standard practice for bilateral official loans and for supplier credits.

Project tying is not without its drawbacks either, notably because of the delays in the evaluation of projects because of the delays in the evaluation of projects suitable for foreign financing. This can even distort the borrower's import structure, as eligible projects may benefit from an otherwise unwarranted priority. Foreign financing has thus been accused of promoting big projects at the expense of grass-roots development; on the other hand, project evaluation is in itself a very useful form of technical assistance.

While project financing was standard practice in the early 1970s, balance-of-payments financing has gained growing importance in recent years. In such cases, the loan is made in support of the borrower's general economic policy, and tying is avoided. Balance-of-payments financing calls for a new sort of risk analysis, since the expectation of reimbursement is based on the success of the borrower's policies rather than on the rate of return for a particular project.

Lenders can be classified as official or private. Official lenders include specialized government agencies as well as international organizations, foremost among which is the World Bank group.

These agencies provide long-term project financing on various terms. Many have established distinct facilities or "windows" in order to offer a range of terms of different concessionality. Adjustment to the needs of recipient countries is further achieved in the form of joint financing among several institutions, with private lenders eventually taking a share of the package.

Suppliers' credits are a first significant class of private loans. They usually benefit from insurance in the lending country. A competition has developed among lenders regarding the terms of these loans, which are influential in developing export markets. A series of negotiations, notably within the OECD, have sought with mitigated success to impose minimal terms in this respect.

Banks have long been active in the financing of international trade and more recently have developed a network of locally incorporated foreign subsidiaries. In the main, however, their most significant activity in respect of foreign debt is their financing of balance-of-payments loans out of Euromarket resources or funds raised in national markets. Because they are untied, but also because they are not concessional, these loans have an original position in the range of financial instruments for external borrowing.

Finally the international bond market also contributes to the financing of developing countries through foreign (that is, placed on a single market) or international (that is, placed on several markets) issues, which may be placed in the public (public offerings) or bought outright by the issuing institutions (private offerings). Few developing countries, however, have gained access to this market yet.

Covering the numerous loans from various sources is a challenging task, and several data systems have been set up, the most operative of which is the World Bank's "Debtor Reporting System." A comprehensive survey of these systems has recently been published by the Bank for International Settlements.[1]

The World Bank's approach is the following:

> External public debt is defined as debt owed to nonresidents repayable in foreign currency, goods or services which has an original or extended maturity of over one year and which is an obligation of:
>
> A public debtor, including the national Government, a political subdivision, or an agency of either, and autonomous public bodies, or,
>
> A private debtor, publicly guaranteed for repayment by a public debtor as defined above.
>
> The [World Debt] tables do not include information about (1) transactions with the International Monetary Fund (IMF); (2) private debt which is not publicly guaranteed; (3) other external obligations for which the amounts and terms have not been agreed; (4) debt repayable at the option of the borrower in local currency; (5) grants; (6) direct investment; and (7) short term capital movements.[2]

The World Bank's survey is based on reports from countries which have received loans from itself or the International Development Association. Ninety-six developing countries currently provide usable data. These are summarized every year in the World Bank's annual report, while more extensive detail is provided in the "World Debt Tables" annual brochure.

The World Bank has also been engaged for some time in a survey of private debts without a public guarantee. These are also covered in the published data of the OECD's Development Assistance Committee (DAC). Members of the DAC provide information about the amounts, the terms, the nature, and the distribution of resources which they transfer to developing countries, whether from private or official sources. Reports include grants and loans with an original maturity of less than a year, direct investment, and so on. Lending information is mostly published on a net basis, that is, drawings minus repayments. The reports thus allow assessment of the total flow of resources to developing countries, but published data are little disaggregated.

A comparison of World Bank and Development Assistance Committee data for 1975[3] shows that the two sources provide closely matching evaluations of the external debts of the eighty-four countries then surveyed by the World Bank. In addition, however, the DAC covers fifty-six other countries, with a debt of $14.5 billion, as well as private debt for the eighty-four countries common to both systems, which amounts to $33.5 billion.

Next to these two general systems, the rise in banking credits led to the development of specific reports.

The World Bank and Morgan Guaranty Trust survey those of the international bond issues or Eurodollar credits which are published in the press. This covers almost all the bond issues on OECD markets, because of publicity requirements, but provides only partial coverage of bank credits, for which publicity is not required. Unpublicized credits are notably those of a small amount, those of short maturity, those which finance weapons trade, and those benefiting new and untested borrowers.

The Bank for International Settlements further compiles data on the external positions of banks in Germany, Belgium and Luxembourg, France, Italy, the Netherlands, the United Kingdom, Sweden, Switzerland (altogether the "European reporting area"), Canada, Japan, the United States, and subsidiaries of U.S. banks in offshore centers. The coverage has been extended since 1978 to banks in Austria, Denmark, and Ireland. All external assets and liabilities are reported, including those relating to trade and the short-term facilities. A maturity breakdown is available for the banks' claims since 1978.

Notes

Introduction

1. David O. Beim, "Rescuing the LDCs," pp. 717-731.

Chapter 1
To the Hilt: The Change in Total Debt

1. Angelos Angelopoulos, "Jusqu'au cou," pp. 37-40.
2. Helen Hughes, Donald B. Keesing, Karsten Laursen, Goran Ohlin, and John D. Shilling, "Prospects for Developing Countries, 1978-1985," mimeographed, IBRD, Washington, November 1977.
3. International Monetary Fund (IMF), Annual Report, 1976, table 9, and 1978, table 8.
4. World Bank, 1978, Annual Report, appendix table 7.

Chapter 2
Commercial Borrowers and Aid-Dependent Countries

1. Data in this section are principally drawn from the World Bank, *World Development Report, 1978.*
2. Ishan Kapur, "The Supply of Eurocurrency Finance to Developing Countries," p. 33; see also "An Analysis of the Supply of Euro-Currency Finance to Developing Countries," pp. 171-188.
3. Barend A. deVries, "The Plight of Small Countries," pp. 6-8.
4. Bangladesh, Colombia, Ethiopia, Ghana, India, Indonesia, Morocco, Korea, Nigeria, Pakistan, Peru, the Philippines, Sudan, Sri Lanka, Thailand, Tunisia, Turkey, Zaire, and the East African Community.
5. David O. Beim, "Rescuing the LDCs," p. 719.

Chapter 3
Borrowers Overexposed: The Casualties

1. David Finch, "Investment Service of Underdeveloped Countries," pp. 70-71.
2. Pierre Dhonte, "Describing External Debt Situations: A Roll-Over Approach," p. 167.

3. World Bank, *World Tables 1976* (Baltimore, Md.: Johns Hopkins University Press, 1976), table 16.

4. United Nations Conference on Trade and Development, Secretariat, Background paper on institutional arrangements for debt renegotiations, Geneva, February 26, 1975, document no. TD/B/C3/AC8/13; and Thomas M. Klein, "Economic Aid through Debt Relief," pp. 17-20, 34-35.

5. Irving S. Friedman, *The Emerging Role of Private Banks in the Developing World.*

6. A. Macleod et al., "The Sick Men of the Euromarkets," *Euromoney*, March 1978.

7. United Nations Conference on Trade and Development, "Manilla Declaration and Programme of Action," mimeographed, Geneva, February 12, 1976, document no. TD/195, p. 22.

8. United Nations Conference on Trade and Development, Secretariat, Background paper on the external debt of developing countries, mimeographed, Geneva, June 30, 1977, document no. TD/AC 2.5, appendix 2.

9. H. van B. Cleveland and W.H. Bruce Brittain, "Are the LDCs in over Their Heads?" p. 745.

10. Robert S. MacNamara, Address to the Board of Governors, Manila, October 4, 1976, p. 17.

11. United Nations Conference on Trade and Development, Secretariat, Background paper on the external debt of developing countries, mimeographed, Geneva, June 30, 1977, document no. TD/AC 2.5, appendix 3.

12. United Nations Conference on Trade and Development: "Manila Declaration," p. 22.

13. Ibid., p. 23.

14. United Nations Conference on Trade and Development, Resolution 94(IV), mimeographed, Geneva, June 10, 1976, document no. TD/RES/94(IV) and Resolution 98(IV), mimeographed, Geneva, June 21, 1976, document no. TD/RES/98(IV).

15. United Nations Conference on Trade and Development, Monthly bulletin, no. 19, Geneva, April 1978.

Chapter 4
Creditors Overextended? The Banks

1. M.M. Ahmad, "The Developing Countries and Access to Financial Markets," pp. 26-30; and Development Committee, "Developing Country Access to Capital Markets," mimeographed, Washington, November 1978.

2. A. Mohammed and F. Saccomanni, "Short Term Banking and Eurocurrency Credits to Developing Countries," pp. 624-625.

3. World Bank, "Borrowing in International Capital Markets," mimeographed, August 1976, table 1.

4. United Nations Conference on Trade and Development, Secretariat, Background paper on bank lending to developing countries, mimeographed, Geneva, June 20, 1977, document no. TD/AC 2.2, tables 3 to 5.

5. "South Korea Loans: Borrower's Market," *The Economist*, April 29, 1978, pp. 130-131.

6. Claude Barroux, "Les Emprunts Russes . . . Soixante Ans Après," *Le Nouvel Economiste*, November 7, 1977, pp. 80-84.

7. David Finch, "Investment Service of Underdeveloped Countries," pp. 62-65.

8. René Larre, "Inflation Mondiale et Activité Bancaire Internationale," p. 15.

9. Declan Duff and Ian Peacock, "Refinancing of Sovereign Debt," p. 73.

10. "International Borrowers Squeeze International Banks," *The Economist*, March 18, 1978, pp. 113-114.

11. IMF Survey, September 4, 1978, p. 263.

12. Stephen Goodman, "How the Big U.S. Banks Really Evaluate Sovereign Risks," pp. 105-110.

13. René Larre: "Le Rôle des Banques dans le Financement des déficits de Balance des Paiements," pp. 41-45.

14. S.M. Yassukovitch, "The Growing Political Threat to International Lending," p. 12.

15. Charles S. Ganoe, "U.S. Banks' International Loans under Scrutiny," pp. 11-13.

16. David O. Beim, "Rescuing the LDCs," p. 725.

17. Ganoe, "U.S. Banks' International Loans under Scrutiny."

18. Irving S. Friedman, "Country Risk: The Lessons of Zaire."

19. Henry Wallich, Statement before the Subcommittee on International Finance of the Committee on Banking, Housing and Urban Affairs, U.S. Senate, August 29, 1977; *Federal Reserve Bulletin*, September 1977, pp. 814-815; and Federal Reserve Bank of New York, "A New Supervisory Approach to Foreign Lending," *Quarterly Review*, Spring 1978, pp. 1-6.

20. *International Herald Tribune*, June 9, 1977, p. 9, and June 11-12, 1977, p. 9; Guillaume Guindey, "Des Projets Monétaires Discutables," pp. 19, 22.

21. Roger A. Hornstein, "Cofinancing of Bank and IDA Projects," pp. 40-43.

Chapter 5
Why Borrow?

1. Nirina Andriamanerasoa and Rajaona Andrianamanjara. "Pour un Développement au Service des Masses des Pays Sous-Développés," pp. 489-491.

2. Cheryl Payer, *The Debt Trap—The IMF and the Third World*, pp. 39, 48.

3. H.B. Chenery and A.M. Strout, "Foreign Assistance and Economic Development," pp. 680-681.

4. Thomas E. Weisskopf, "The Impact of Foreign Capital Inflows on Domestic Savings in Underdeveloped Countries," p. 25.

5. Ronald Findlay, "The 'Foreign Exchange Gap' and Growth in Developing Economies," p. 719.

6. Hans O. Schmidt, "Development Assistance: The View from Bretton Woods," p. 586.

7. J.P. Hayes, "Long-Run Growth and Debt Servicing Problems," pp. 154-192; A. Quayum, "Long-Term Economic Criteria for Foreign Loans," pp. 358-369; R.J. Ball, "Capital Imports and Economic Growth: Paradoxy or Orthodoxy?"; and B.F. Massell, "Exports, Capital Imports and Economic Growth."

8. David Finch, "Investment Service of Underdeveloped Countries," pp. 62-67.

9. Claudio Loser, "External Debt Management and Balance of Payments Policies," p. 176.

Chapter 6
Borrowing Capacity: Soft Terms or Rapid Growth

1. P.A. Wellons, "Borrowing by Developing Countries on the Euro-Currency Market."

2. Evsey D. Domar, "The Effects of Foreign Investment on the Balance of Payments," pp. 805-826.

Chapter 7
A New Relationship

1. International Monetary Fund, "Direction of Trade," *Annual 1971-1977.*

2. General Agreement on Tariffs and Trade, "Le Commerce International en 1976-77," Geneva, 1977, table 7.

3. The seventy-five nonoil developing countries surveyed in the 1977 World Debt Tables recorded net public borrowings of $8.5 billion in 1973 and added $9.6 billion to reserves. In 1975 they borrowed $20.1 billion and drew $2.2 billion from reserves, for a total shift of $23.4 billion (World Bank, "World Debt Tables, 1977," vol. 1, p. 41.)

4. International Monetary Fund, *Annual Report 1977*, table 9.

5. René Larre: "Le Rôle des Banques dans le Financement des Déficits de Balance des Paiements," pp. 44-45.

Chapter 8
Walking the Tightrope

1. International Monetary Fund, *Annual Report 1977*, table 6.

2. Ibid., p. 20.

3. Robert S. MacNamara, Address to the Board of Governors, Washington, D.C., September 26, 1977, p. 15.

Appendix A
The Mechanics of Debt

1. Ewsey D. Domar, "The Effects of Foreign Investment on the Balance of Payments," pp. 805-826.

Appendix D
Statistical Sources

1. Bank for International Settlements, Manual on Statistics compiled by International Organisations on Countries' External Indebtedness, mimeographed, Baste, BIS, March 1979, 109 pages.

2. World Bank, "World Debt Tables, 1977," vol. 1, p. 50.

3. Organization for Economic Cooperation and Development, "Development Co-Operation: Efforts and Policies of Members of the Development Assistance Committee, 1977 Review" (Paris: OECD, 1977), statistical appendix E.

Bibliography

Ahmad, M.M. "The Developing Countries and Access to Financial Markets," *Finance and Development*, December 1976, pp. 26-30.

Andriamanerasoa, N., and Andrianamanjara, R. "Pour un Développement au Service des Masses des Pays Sous-Développés," *Revue Tiers Monde*, July-September 1977, pp. 481-92.

Angelopoulos, A. "Jusqu'au Cou," *Cérès*, French edition, September-October 1977, pp. 37-40.

Ball, R.J. "Capital Imports and Economic Growth; Paradoxy or Orthodoxy?" *Kyklos* 15 (1962): 610-23, pt. 3, and 18 (1965): 139-40, pt. 1.

Beim, D.O. "Rescuing the LDCs," *Foreign Affairs*, July 1977, pp. 717-51.

Chenery, H.B., and Strout, A.M. "Foreign Assistance and Economic Development," *American Economic Review*, December 1966, pp. 679-733.

Cleveland, H. van B., and Bruce Brittain, W.H. "Are the LDCs in over Their Heads?" *Foreign Affairs*, July 1977, pp. 732-50.

de Vries, B.A. "The Plight of Small Countries," *Finance and Development*, September 1973, pp. 6-8.

Dhonte, P. "Describing External Debt Situations: A Roll-Over Approach," International Monetary Fund Staff Papers, March 1975, pp. 159-86.

Domar, E.D. "The Effects of Foreign Investment on the Balance of Payments," *American Economic Review*, December 1950, pp. 805-26.

Duff, D., and Peacock, I. "Refinancing of Sovereign Debt," *The Banker*, January 1978, pp. 69-75.

Federal Reserve Board of New York: "A New Supervisory Approach to Foreign Lending," *Quarterly Review*, Spring 1978, pp. 1-6.

Finch, D. "Investment Service of Underdeveloped Countries," International Monetary Fund Staff Papers, September 1951, pp. 60-85.

Findlay, R. "The 'Foreign Exchange Gap' and Growth in Developing Countries," in *Trade, Balance of Payments and Growth*, Papers in International Economics, C.P. Kindleberger, J.N. Bhagwati, R.W. Jones, R.A. Mundell, and J. Vanek, eds. (Amsterdam: North-Holland, 1971), pp. 168-82.

Friedman, I.S. *The Emerging Role of Private Banks in the Developing World* (New York: Citicorp, 1977).

______. "Country Risk: The Lessons of Zaire," *The Banker*, February 1978.

Ganoe, C.S. "U.S. Banks' International Loans under Scrutiny," *Euromoney*, March 1976, pp. 11-13.

Goodman, S. "How the Big U.S. Banks Really Evaluate Sovereign Risk," *Euromoney*, February 1977, pp. 105-110.

Guindey, G. "Des Projets Monétaires Discutables," *Le Monde*, June 21, 1977, pp. 19, 22.

Hayes, J.P. "Long-Run Growth and Debt Servicing Problems," in D. Avramovic et al., *Economic Growth and External Debt* (Baltimore, Md.: Johns Hopkins University Press, IBRD, 1964), pp. 154-92.

Hornstein, R.A. "Cofinancing of Bank and IDA Projects," *Finance and Development*, June 1977, pp. 40-45.

Kapur, I. "The Supply of Eurocurrency Finance to Developing Countries," *Finance and Development*, September 1977, pp. 32-36.

______. "An Analysis of the Supply of Euro-Currency Finance to Developing Countries," *Oxford Bulletin of Economics and Statistics*, August 1977, pp. 171-88.

Klein, T.M. "Economic Aid through Debt Relief," *Finance and Development*, September 1973, pp. 17-20, 34-35.

Larre, R. "Inflation Mondiale et Activité Bancaire Internationale," *Le Monde*, June 26, 1977, p. 15.

______. "Le Rôle des Banques dans le Financement des Deficits de Balance des Paiements," *Banque*, January 1978, pp. 41-45.

Loser, C. "External Debt Management and Balance of Payments Policies," International Monetary Fund Staff Papers, March 1977, pp. 168-92.

Massell, B.F. "Exports, Capital Imports, and Economic Growth," *Kyklos* 17 (1964):627-35, pt. 4.

Mohammed, A., and Saccomanni, F. "Short Term Banking and Eurocurrency Credits to Developing Countries," International Monetary Fund Staff Papers, September 1973, pp. 612-38.

Payer, C. *The Debt Trap—The IMF and the Third World* (Baltimore, Md.: Penguin Books, 1974).

Quayum, A. "Long-Term Economic Criteria for Foreign Loans," *Economic Journal*, June 1966, pp. 358-69.

Schmidt, H.O. "Development Assistance: The View from Bretton Woods," *Public Policy* 4 (1973):585-600.

United Nations Conference on Trade and Development. Background paper on institutional arrangements for debt renegotiations, mimeographed, Geneva, February 26, 1975, document no. TD/B/C3/AC8/13.

______. "Manila Declaration and Programme of Action," mimeographed, Geneva, February 12, 1976, document no. TD/195.

______. Background paper on the external debt of developing countries, mimeographed, Geneva, June 30, 1977, document no. TD/AC 2.5.

______. Background paper on bank lending to developing countries, mimeographed, Geneva, June 20, 1977, document no. TD/AC 2/2.

Weisskopf, T.E. "The Impact of Foreign Capital Inflows on Domestic Savings in Underdeveloped Countries," *Journal of International Economics* 2 (1972):25-38

Wellons, P.A. *Borrowing by Developing Countries on the Euro-Currency Market* (Paris: OECD, 1977).
World Bank. "Prospects for Developing Countries, 1978-1985," mimeographed, IBRD, Washington, November 1977.
______. *World Development Report, 1978*, Washington, 1978.
Yassukovitch, S.M. "The Growing Political Threat to International Lending," *Euromoney*, April 1976, pp. 10-13.

Index

Index

About the Author

Pierre Dhonte holds the doctorate in economics from the University of Paris, France. He served as an instructor with the University of Paris before joining the staff of the International Monetary Fund from 1972 to 1977. In that capacity he first became acquainted with external debt problems and visited a number of developing countries in Africa, Asia, and the Middle East. He was working with the French Caisse Centrale de Cooperation Economique when he wrote this book.